Destructive Myths in Family Therapy

Destructive Myths in Family Therapy

How to Overcome Barriers to Communication by Seeing and Saying – A Humanistic Perspective

Daniela Kramer-Moore and Michael Moore

WILEY-BLACKWELL

A John Wiley & Sons, Ltd., Publication

This edition first published 2012
© 2012 John Wiley & Sons, Ltd.

Wiley-Blackwell is an imprint of John Wiley & Sons, formed by the merger of Wiley's global Scientific, Technical and Medical business with Blackwell Publishing.

Registered office: John Wiley & Sons, Ltd, The Atrium, Southern Gate, Chichester, West Sussex, PO19 8SQ, UK

Editorial offices: 350 Main Street, Malden, MA 02148-5020, USA
9600 Garsington Road, Oxford, OX4 2DQ, UK
The Atrium, Southern Gate, Chichester, West Sussex, PO19 8SQ, UK

For details of our global editorial offices, for customer services, and for information about how to apply for permission to reuse the copyright material in this book please see our website at www.wiley.com/wiley-blackwell.

The right of Daniela Kramer-Moore and Michael Moore to be identified as the authors of this work has been asserted in accordance with the UK Copyright, Designs and Patents Act 1988.

Library of Congress Cataloging-in-Publication Data

Kramer-Moore, Daniela.
   Destructive myths in family therapy : how to overcome barriers to communication by seeing and saying : a humanistic perspective / Daniela Kramer-Moore and Michael Moore.
      p. ; cm.
   Includes bibliographical references and index.
   ISBN 978-0-470-66701-9 (hardback : alk. paper) – ISBN 978-0-470-66700-2 (pbk. : alk. paper)
   I. Moore, Michael, 1942 Sept. 19- II. Title.
   [DNLM: 1. Family Therapy–methods.   2. Communication.   3. Family–psychology. 4. Family Relations.   5. Humanism. WM 430.5.F2]
   616.89′156–dc23

                                                                                          2011053425

A catalogue record for this book is available from the British Library.

Wiley also publishes its books in a variety of electronic formats. Some content that appears in print may not be available in electronic books

Set in 10.5/13pt Minion by Aptara Inc., New Delhi, India

Printed in Singapore by Ho Printing Singapore Pte Ltd

1   2012

With love to our children: Gilad, Karen, Ofer, Rafi, Yotam, and Yuval

Contents

Preface

In our therapy sessions, we see families in their dramas: between spouses, parents and children, vis-à-vis extended family members, between siblings. Even though most claim that they want to live in harmony with their immediate family, they keep bickering, miscommunicating, hurting one another, and ruining relationships. It is logical to presume that every young couple wants only happiness for themselves and for their future children, without causing or feeling pain and crises. Yet as therapists who meet families in pain we see them systematically destroying family events, living under much stress, ending up in divorce or even worse: chronic aversion, bringing up children with behavioral problems. Erich Fromm, social psychologist, psychoanalyst and humanistic philosopher, (1977, p. 8) suggested that "Man seeks for drama and excitement; when he cannot get satisfaction on a higher level, he creates for himself the drama of destruction." Even those who do not want dramas, may have no choice if they do not know any better, for they have brought from their families of origin patterns of competition, one-upmanship, lack of trust in others, or a lack of awareness of their inner world. Often when they try to share or understand what is happening to them, they resort to well-practiced patterns of blaming and quarreling, ending up even more distant from each other and less capable of mutual trust. To make things more difficult, in order to progress to a mode of communication that is more nourishing, it is not enough for one person to speak effectively. Both parent figures, who serve as models for their children, need to learn how to give up dysfunctional communication patterns and to adopt a new language of trust, empathy, authenticity, and mutual respect toward each other and toward their children. Thus, we find family and couple therapy as the first step towards improving the quality of family life, with the therapist acting as a communication instructor and mediator.

In therapy both the therapist and the family are involved in a team of equals, all bringing what they know best to this project. The therapist brings knowledge of functional communication, ability to see interpersonal processes, an empathic personality, patience and tolerance, thus serving as both guide and supporter in an intricate, difficult task. However, this does not make the family change. The adults (or the couple) bring their pain and expose it as sincerely as they can, as well as honest motivation for starting to change not each other but themselves. Both of these ingredients are necessary for therapeutic changes to occur.

With this aim in mind, we offer this book to students and practitioners of family therapy, social work, and educational counseling, as well as to those members of the public who are interested in improving family communication, thereby advancing intimacy within the family unit. The need for such improvement is beyond doubt, when close to one-half of all marriages in the Western world end in divorce.

Screaming infants, totally absorbed by their immediate plight, communicate without considering the emotional needs of their listeners. We expect physical, cognitive, and emotional development to help them turn gradually into more mature individuals who are aware of the norms and expectations that pertain to the use of verbal and non-verbal communication. Increased control of vocal cords and of other organs used for communication comes naturally and needs no parental guidance. Children need to learn, however, how to use those organs, first from parents, then from an ever-widening circle of other socializing agents. All of these teachers can impart only what they know and (especially) what they practice, so that one generation of dysfunctional communicators is likely to breed another. The residues of the poor, sometimes pathogenic, communication skills one picks up during childhood last for a lifetime. Those not taught to surpass the phase of self-centeredness and lack the skill to be empathic will pay a price: they cannot have a relationship characterized by intimacy and open communication, for having hurt their audience a number of times, the latter will keep their safe distance.

Many may have noticed that they are both causing and experiencing pain related to their interpersonal communication, and that while they can have quite satisfactory conversations with strangers, talks with the most significant persons in their social environment are not successful. They feel that their words make them fail, but they lack the skill to change. They may suddenly realize that they sound like their parents, but have no tools for applying a different communication style. The intent of this book is to assist their therapists in giving them these tools.

Part I deals with the recognition of dysfunctionality and the basic steps of family therapy. Chapters 1 and 2 introduce readers to the importance of *seeing* the needs and the pains of one's family (no matter how uncomfortable it makes them feel) and to the pathogenic consequences of failing to see them. Chapter 3 outlines the major goals and stages of family therapy, and suggests an analysis of some themes that are likely to appear in most families. In Chapter 4 we stop between *seeing* and *saying* in order to help therapists apply their ability to stop and reflect on the family process, to establish more functional communication. Each chapter contains several highly detailed therapy activities for working with couples and families at every stage of therapy.

Part II of this book is organized around six of the most common pathological family processes, each illustrated by analyses of numerous frequently heard myths and *sayings*. When persistently used within the family setting, the latter undermine closeness, openness and intimacy between spouses or between parents and children. The analysis that follows each saying looks into the different possible motivations that underlie them; the therapy activities accompanying each chapter provide ways to combat them and to replace them with functional alternatives.

The nineteenth century French literary critic Sainte-Beuve has been quoted saying that critics' first duty is to know how to read, and their second duty is to teach others to do the same (Lee, ca. 1910). We shall borrow from him and apply this maxim to (family) therapists: First learn to see and to listen, then teach these skills to others.

Acknowledgments

We would like to thank Darren Reed and Karen Shield at Wiley-Blackwell for their help and encouragement.

We gratefully acknowledge the assistance we received from the University of Warwick Psychology Department and from the University of Warwick Library's Department of Document Supply. Our thanks are also due to our clients and students, who have taught us so much.

The illustrations on pages 1, 5, 18, 33, 73, 77, 94, 111, 126, 142, 155, and 169 are by Ruth Mohos.

The illustration on p. 52 is by Tamara Aloni.

Part I

Seeing

The Choices we Make

Eyes have they, but they see not. (Psalms 115:5)

Fay Weldon's short story (1981), *Man With No Eyes*, is a goldmine of patho-logical family processes (*PFPs*): A downtrodden, anxiety-ridden mother, afraid of her domineering husband, is determined to preserve her marriage

---

Destructive Myths in Family Therapy: How to Overcome Barriers to Communication by Seeing and Saying – A Humanistic Perspective, First Edition. Daniela Kramer-Moore and Michael Moore.
© 2012 John Wiley & Sons, Ltd. Published 2012 by John Wiley & Sons, Ltd.

for the sake of their two young daughters. The story gains special poignancy through repeated references to a scary, mysterious *man with no eyes*, symbolizing both her father (who had deserted his wife and daughter), her husband, who is totally blind to his family's needs, and herself, who ignores the harm that will come to her daughters if she stays in her pathogenic marriage.

Unseeing spouses and parents are not a rarity in real life; they are certainly familiar to those engaged in family therapy. Many people do not see. The consequences of such metaphorical blindness can be far reaching: when there is no insight into our own motives (and into those of others), we are on auto-pilot, we repeat our own past behaviors, dysfunctional as they may have been, unquestioningly copy the acts and opinion of others, bring unhealthy patterns of behavior from our family of origin to our nuclear family, all this without examining what builds relationships and what destroys them. Unless we stop and reflect, we cannot learn from past mistakes, and so we find ourselves in the same painful situations again and again.

It is our contention that such blindness (serving as the subject of Chapter 1) is an acquired response. For some individuals it serves as a defense against painful involvement, so common in human relationships. For them not seeing is first a choice, then a habit. Many others use blindness by default, having been surrounded by unseeing adults in their formative years. This type of learning is of special importance in the life of families. To a large extent, man's being a link in the human chain, "one segment of history," as Erikson (1963, pp. 268–269) put it, is based on our ability to carry out observational learning or modeling. This highly effective and ubiquitous social mechanism was defined by Hogg and Vaughan (2011, p. 651) as "The tendency for a person to reproduce the actions, attitudes and emotional responses exhibited by a real-life or symbolic model." Having observed our parent figures during the early stages of our life, each of us mirrors, to some extent, an internalized version of them. In our turn, we use the same mechanism to shape the generation that follows us: what children see and copy from their parents' conduct, shapes their behavior toward the world in general, and toward their spouse and offspring, in particular. Such shaping is essential for the continuation of culture in all its aspects. It is also the vehicle for the *transgenerational* transmission of PFPs.

Here is how Erich Fromm described this facet of the principle underlying transgenerationality: "The child is usually defeated by the superior strength of the adult, but the defeat does not remain without consequences; it would seem to activate a tendency to overcome the defeat by doing actively what one was forced to endure passively: to rule when one had to obey; to beat when one was beaten; in short, to do what one was forced to suffer, or to do what one was forbidden to do" (Fromm, 1977, p. 317). Alice Miller, a Swiss psychologist and psychoanalyst, also commented on the transmission of PFPs from one generation to the next: "If these people [who were traumatized, as children] become parents, they will then often direct acts of revenge for their mistreatment in childhood against their own children, whom they use as scapegoats" (Miller, 1990, p. 282). Virginia Satir, a key figure in family therapy (1988, p. 212), used the term "family blueprint" in this context, to emphasize the crucial influence of personal history in parenting: "I have heard parents lament," she wrote, "'I did not want to be like my mother and father, but I am turning out exactly like them.'" Of course, we must point out that not only painful, dysfunctional behaviors are copied from the adults we meet in childhood. In functional families we learn from them to be kind, thoughtful, and empathic; we can imitate a father's sensitivity, a mother's humor, and a grandparent's endless patience, as well.

Knowing that our children grow up "in our own image", that our behavior towards and in front of them is noted, stored, and eventually retrieved is only one aspect of *seeing*. The blindness vs. seeing issue concerns individuals' responsibility for being aware of the needs of other members of their social sphere, as well: first and foremost other family members (though in this book we focus on the latter, circles widen from friends, through colleagues, to society at large). For individuals to be able to gain insight into their own situation and to help themselves and their families (on their own or through a therapist) they need first to identify what troubles them, then to arrive at sounder structure and more congruent communication, and to become aware of the existence of healthy family patterns. For spouses to be able to avoid drawing their children into their marital conflicts, even when they are under stress, they need to comprehend the significance of a healthy spousal coalition; to avoid power struggles, to know that any private victory is a defeat for the family system, they need to understand the value of equality and teamwork. And (to return to parenthood) only those parents who see that the function of families is to satisfy every member's needs for security, affection and appreciation, are in the position to ask themselves and each other, whether the family does indeed provide such satisfaction; only self-aware parents can respect their children and their children's needs, rather than use them for their own needs; only they are able to encourage a sibling coalition, instead of setting their children against each other; only they can nourish them during the critical years and let go of them when they mature.

The first part of this book therefore attempts to help the reader identify what happens to and around individuals in their family circle, to encourage them to try out various alternatives, to give them more choices, more conscious control over relationships. It is our position that one can choose not to continue on a dysfunctional path, one can unlearn what has been learned.

1

Blindness, or With Eyes Wide Shut

Go, you seer, flee away. (Amos 7:12)

It takes time for newborns to develop the ability to see the world around them, to focus on stationary objects, to follow the moving ones, and to use the information contained in patterns and colors. Developing another kind of seeing, unrelated to the optic nerve, also takes time. Here we are referring to the ability to look into oneself and into others, to see – somewhat paradoxically – of all things, those that are not apparent to the eye. The paradoxical nature of metaphorical seeing was made even more blatant by the existentialist psychotherapist Irwin Yalom (1993, p. 163), one of whose characters says that "sometimes I see better with closed eyes," perhaps because appearances always hide some underlying stratum. Such non-physical, non-literal seeing has important implications for both intra- and interpersonal situations.

In the intra-personal realm many individuals have the ability to arrive at an understanding of themselves through conscious reflection. For some others the clear perception of their own needs and drives may occur sud- denly, as in a flash. These two types of seeing respectively correspond to the conscious and preconscious layers of personality. Yet the cornerstone of all psychodynamic theories, such as Freud's or Jung's, is the emphasis on unconscious motivation. The latter implies that a considerable portion of our behavior is driven by motives to which we are blind. Psychotherapy is concerned with the gaining of *insight*, or the bringing to light of hidden, dark corners of one's life (see Chapter 3).

When it comes to social relationships, any inability to see oneself tends to spread to significant others: we cannot see others without first seeing ourselves. A further complication occurs when a person's inability or un- willingness to see leaves unsatisfied the surrounding persons' need to be seen. The gap that occurs may have far-reaching consequences: Murray Bowen, a psychiatrist who was one of the pioneers of family therapy, threw light on the family dynamics that made individuals within families choose pathogenic coping mechanisms, rather than look at the underlying family currents (Kerr and Bowen, 1988).

Seeing one's own needs and motives or those of others involves several stages. First one must stop. This is not an easy undertaking, for we tend to continue our ongoing activities, in spite of various internal and external interruptions. As is the case with the related tendency toward homeostasis (discussed in Chapter 5), this inclination is often very useful, for it keeps us on track. However, occasionally it also prevents us from examining our experiences, from giving ourselves an account of what is happening to us and around us. So first of all – stop. Then reflect. This is another difficult task, requiring conscious effort. Reflection (a form of introspection) involves self-questioning and re-examining one's emotions, thoughts and behaviors; as such, it forms the basis of learning about ourselves and about our relationship to our social environment. Bennett-Levy (2003, p. 18) considered this capacity to re-present and analyze past, present, and future events as a unique human skill. Only after having thus stopped and thought reflectively, can one claim to have embarked on the process of gaining insight.

Keeping achieved insights to oneself offers limited benefits within the family context: one must put to use such self-observations by acting upon them and by sharing them with one's intimate circle. A circular process is likely to be set in motion, for the more one shares knowledge about oneself with significant others, the more they will be ready to share their insights, resulting in increased closeness.

Family dynamics, similarly to other interpersonal situations, may be characterized by the type of communication that typically takes place in them (more about family communication patterns on pp. 74–75). Communication, however, is not an entirely transparent process. Every human activity conveys meanings at several levels: concrete and abstract, manifest and latent, iconic and symbolic. Uninvolved, observant outsiders are more likely to see both overt and covert levels than the concerned parties, for the former are not threatened by connotations and associations. Messages used within the family have (at least) three layers of meaning (Kramer-Moore and Moore, 2002, pp. 25–31. For a thorough discussion of the possible interpretation of messages see Eco, 1990). We shall refer to these as an overt, manifest meaning, visible to all (Layer A); a hidden meaning, both intended and disguised by its sender (Layer B); and a deep layer, to which the portrayer is blind, and which is visible to some observers, hidden to others (Layer C; see Box 1.1). Valesio (1980, pp. 41–42) referred to the mechanism underlying the latter as one "that speaks through the speaker-writer, often against his intention." These three layers are analogous to the public, hidden, and blind regions, respectively, of the Johari window of self-awareness (see Luft, 1969). We consider the gaps among the three as the source of dysfunctional communication.

Box 1.1 Circles within circles

Fairy tales are a perfect source for illustrating layers of meaning; not unlike myths, these stories for children contain more than what meets the eye. In his analysis of several popular tales (such as *Jack and the*

(*continued*)

Beanstalk, Little Red Riding Hood, and *Cinderella*) the psychologist Bruno Bettelheim (1976) used psychoanalytic techniques to reveal their covert meaning; others (e.g. Tatar, 1992) applied tools taken from additional disciplines to go beyond the surface message delivered by bedtime stories.

We shall use Grimm's (1944) *St. Joseph in the Forest* tale to exemplify the three layers:

Layer A: a mother loves her selfish daughter rather than her well-behaved, pious one. Disguised as a beggar, St. Joseph discovers their true mettle; rewards the good daughter, kills the bad one and punishes their mother.

Layer B: human judgment is erroneous, but God "tries the reins and the heart." Or, we should be always considerate and giving to others, since we do not know who has the power to punish us.

Layer C: a mother may play favorites with her children, as long as she prefers the good one. Furthermore, as a mode of behavior, self-sacrifice is preferred to self-preservation, and even to fair sharing of food. Only the professional reader will see that both of these Layer C messages are pathological from a psychological point of view.

Dangers, Taboos, and Punishments

Seeing is a potentially dangerous exercise: the readiness to look at some previously well-camouflaged areas of our life, and thereby gain the opportunity to employ healthier coping strategies can have painful consequences. Making others see is no less dangerous. The often violent rejection of seers has been told many times both throughout history and literature; it has continued in some modern societies, where those who criticize the establishment or do not turn a blind-eye to corruption can find themselves in physical danger. We know of entire political systems that have invested incredible amounts of energy to prevent their citizens from seeing: the Third Reich disguised its extermination camps as work camps; the Soviet Union flooded its mass media with slogans and lies. Anyone who dared to see presented a threat and was silenced. Seeing and saying – the theme that underlies this book – is a particularly apt description of what whistleblowers do (apologies for mixing metaphors), quite often exposing themselves to danger by saying what they see.

Within smaller, more intimate groups, such as the family, similar processes occur. Some family members are blind, others can see in varying degrees. Some keep quiet, while a few have both the courage and the energy to speak up. The latter often take on the role of the Identified Patient (IP): This is the symptom-bearing family member (the "official patient" in Nichols and Schwartz, 2006, p. 446), whose asking for help may indicate the presence of an underlying family conflict. In individual therapy it is naturally the IP who is treated, often having been sent by the family, whose overt message is: "There is something wrong with this person, s/he needs to be changed!" But there is an underlying, layer C message, as well: "This person sees too much, make her more blind to the cause of family pain!" Let us hasten to add that IPs can be as blind as the rest of the family to the connection of their plight to some dysfunctionality in the family, yet their involuntary cry for help can draw the therapist's attention to its systemic source.

Identified Patients

We shall diverge for a moment, to point out that the practice of family therapy – not unlike other theory driven endeavors – does not rest on a single, universally accepted psychological theory. Take, for example, the meanings given to the so called Identified Patient by different schools of thought. The founder of structural family therapy Salvador Minuchin (1974; Minuchin and Fishman, 1981), along with other proponents of system theories, suggested that the IP expresses the dysfunctionality of his or her family. Therefore a reduction of the IP's symptoms is made possible only through a change in the entire system. According to the Satir model of family therapy (Satir, 1983) the IP's symptoms are an SOS call regarding family pain. Virginia Satir is also a system theorist: "Each member in the system is a most significant factor in keeping the system going as it is or changing it. Discovering your part in the system and seeing others' parts is an exciting, although sometimes painful, experience" (Satir, 1988, p. 136). NIDA (the American National Institute on Drug Abuse) has taken a similar position: in their publication on family therapy for adolescent drug abuse (2008) it is suggested that the IP (in this case the drug-abusing adolescent) is branded by the family as the problem, not recognizing that the real problem lies in the family's habitual and rigid patterns of interaction. Other theorists, especially those identified with constructivism (e.g. Seikkula, 2002), reject the direct and necessary connection between the IP's symptoms and the family's underlying conflicts. Instead, they suggest that the lives of families are, to a large extent, shaped by the stories and beliefs they construct about themselves. These constructions (not unlike the destructive sayings and myths treated in Part II of this book) can be extremely powerful, hindering the family from using alternative options and functional coping mechanisms. Michael White's (2007) narrative therapy approach is an attempt to rewrite these stories, so the family can, as a group, take control over their life, rather than letting the symptoms control it. The constructivist approach recognizes the embeddedness of the family in a larger cultural context which both contributes to the family's construction of the conflict that distresses it, and is continuously constructed by it.

Our clinical experience leads us to believe that IPs, be they children or adults, are inescapably connected to their intimate social circle. If they go into therapy by themselves, at best they can cut themselves off; at worst their family ties them down and uses them to further its own agenda. A systemic approach is needed, where the family dynamic is unraveled and functional communication within the family is established so that the IP can stop being the outlet for family pain. The IP is not the only one who gains from this development: the rest of the group can go on with their lives without feeling obligated to sacrifice themselves "for the sake of the family."

A Continuum of Blindness

As dangerous as seeing may be, the prices of blindness are far greater. The psychologically blind harm both themselves and their significant others: they are not in touch with reality, accept no responsibility for things that do not work, and therefore are unable to correct them. Though they may be physically surrounded by people, emotionally they are alone. What they do not see starts with their own traits and behaviors: "Me, a control freak? You must be kidding!" Blindness then extends to others: their spouse's misery, their daughter's anorexia, their son's depression, another relative's sexual abuse.

Before continuing we must confess to a bias, already apparent in the last passage. Our point of view in this book in general, and vis-à-vis blindness in particular, is influenced by the Western, democratic societies we live in, and by our orientation as humanistic psychologists. We are aware of the fact that these ideologies are not shared by all (see, for example, Dwairy, 2006) and that, under certain circumstances, not seeing may be preferable to seeing. This might especially be the case in cultures that promote reticence, reserve or shyness, and where not conforming to these values may endanger both one's physical self and psychological well-being (more on this in Chapter 3).

Being able to see is not a matter of all-or-nothing, so we can point out several stages along a continuum:

Total blindness

When interviewing families in which at least one member is miserable, we commonly hear such opening declarations: "We have a great marriage!"; "We treat/love all our children equally!"; "I have no problems"; "Everyone says I'm such a great mom." These individuals see and blame only the external world. They typically take no responsibility for internal processes and do not invest any energy in attempts to understand what lies behind some family members' misery. Disturbing events are all attributed to sources external to self (an example of situational rather than dispositional attribution; see Aronson, Wilson, and Akert, 2010, p. 439). With their self-centeredness, such blind family members are likely to have poor interpersonal relationships, regard those who obstruct them as either bad, manipulative, or stupid, without seeing their own contribution to frustrating events. To protect themselves from the acute suffering that would result from seeing, they refuse to let go of their defense mechanisms, condemning themselves and those around them to chronic misery, with no hope for development and change.

The totally blind – often anxiety ridden and suffering from low self-esteem – do not seek help, but occasionally they are dragged into family therapy by another, better sighted family member. They are likely to become resistant clients who do not benefit from therapy, often adding the therapist to their black list. A frequently heard statement from them is "I don't believe in psychology," whose Layer C is "Don't show me anything that can hurt."

Tunnel vision

Though they also look only for external causes and tend not to realize their own contribution to family suffering, some people may be aware of the existence of a general family problem: for example, "All children are ungrateful"; "No marriage is perfect, so why keep talking about it?"; "They don't appreciate me out of envy." Each of these speakers admits the existence of a problem but blames someone else for it. Such blaming inevitably entails the belittling of others, thus causing further conflict (more on this in Chapter 8). Yet the recognition that something is wrong may bring such individuals to seek professional help, which is the first step towards regaining sight.

Partial vision

"I see the problem. I realize that I'm at least partially responsible for it." Yet with these persons the pain of this realization (as in "I ruin every relationship I enter") is so great, that they cannot afford to look at the underlying causes either in self or in others. Instead of healthy coping, the process is likely to stop at self-loathing or even to lead to depression. They drown in their misery, unable to see the other, including the other's share in this process. Neither can they analyze what it is in their behavior that contributes to family distress. This stage involves mourning, a feeling of great loss, including the loss of safety that would result from being able to blame others for one's own lack of success. As with other instances of mourning, one has to go through several stages until acceptance is reached. When this partial insight is gained in therapy, the process cannot stop here, for the losses outweigh the gains.

Broad vistas

When individuals can see both their contribution and that of the other, when they are able to discern what in their behavior triggers unpleasant, unwanted responses, they are on the right path. At this stage they are able to assume responsibility for their share in the family's stressful dynamics without blaming themselves or others. The acceptance of imperfection and the ability to perceive the systemic aspects of family life are characteristic also of individuals who have gained much from therapy. Their voyage is not over, for they may still benefit from learning healthy coping mechanisms, for *seeing* and *saying* are both necessary for the maintenance of healthy relationships.

Clear vision

This is probably an unattainable goal. We all have our blind spots; we all resort occasionally to the use of defense mechanisms. It is only befitting, therefore, to become acquainted with Carl Rogers' (1972) rather utopian description of *The Person of Tomorrow*. Rogers, a founder and key-figure of humanistic psychology, emphasized this emerging person's awareness of and sensitivity to both the thoughts and feelings of self and of others. This ability to see both inwards and outwards is accompanied by a rejection of "sham, facade, or pretense", as well as by openness to experience. The New Person is neither perfect nor strives for perfection. Instead, s/he is "a searching person, without any neat answers," who is communicative, spontaneous, authentic (more about authenticity in Chapter 6). Clearer vision brings with it efficient coping, which is not subject to myths. Clear-sighted persons are connected to the here-and-now without becoming defensive. In Bowen's terminology (1976a), they have solid, rather than pseudo-selves, so they are able to bring authenticity into their interpersonal relationships. As a result, they tend to make healthier choices: invest mostly in satisfying relationships, and divest themselves from those that are chronically frustrating. Every new meaningful interaction is used to further one's insight and empathy towards others.

Surprise, Surprise!

Surprises, particularly unpleasant ones, are usually a result of blindness. Parents are surprised when their child kills self or others; spouses are surprised when their partner cheats, leaves, or asks for divorce; neighbors are surprised, when they cannot believe that "he has done it". "Didn't they see it coming?" we are tempted to ask. But then all of these are blind, for one reason or another. In his book *Blindness*, Nobel laureate Jose Saramago (1998) quoted an old proverb: "No one is more blind than those who don't want to see!" Indeed, those who resort to blindness in order to protect themselves from pain – and that includes all of us, to one extent or another – refuse to acknowledge what is either cognitively or emotionally disturbing. Apparently we are all able to perceive something at one level, only to reject it at another (see the literature on subliminal perception, reviewed in Merikle and Daneman, 1998). And so parents can ignore teachers' observations about their children's behavior, disregard the latter's isolation and near muteness, the misery they project, their dislike for themselves, their ennui, eating disorders or truancy. "It's just a stage, it will pass, it's normal, all their friends do it."

In contrast to those who do not allow themselves to see, the blindness of some is an acquired disability. The transgenerational nature of this PFP is apparent: We all tend to copy the behavior of our parents. Growing up in a family where one or both adults are psychologically blind, where instead of talking matters out, painful issues simply become "invisible", will transmit this unhealthy coping mechanism from one generation to the other. In his description of the transgenerational aspects of family dysfunction, Bowen (1976a, p. 83) suggested that the severity of impairment is even likely to increase in successive generations. When in therapy, such individuals are surprised not only by what they can now see, but also by the discovery that they now possess such a skill of sight. In family therapy sessions clients frequently exclaim: "I can't believe I didn't see that myself!" or "How could I've been so blind!"

Individuals' failure to see an approaching event, that is to say the fact that they "didn't see it coming," is the direct result of both poor insight and poor communication. Here again the tight connection between *seeing* and *saying* becomes apparent: surprises can be avoided by reflecting on processes, looking one step ahead, discussing these seeing processes with meaningful others. Authentic, direct communication serves as a mirror that reflects at least some parts of perceived reality. Therefore, if one is surprised at a failure (or success) of any member of the intimate social circle, if one is unprepared for what is now happening, this signals failure to see and to engage others in a meaningful dialogue. The task of the therapist begins with helping family members gradually see, and extends to identifying the communication gaps and the use of PFPs, empathizing with the pain of seeing, and expressing acceptance and warmth towards both the IP and his/her family. Therapists have a great advantage: being distanced from the family group, they can see the larger picture and its underlying dynamics, without involvement, pain or anxiety. The Milan model of family therapy (see, for example, Goldenberg and Goldenberg, 2008, pp. 291–292) has taken the concept of distancing, for the purpose of seeing, a step further. The assumption is that the therapist, who is directly involved with the family, also develops blind-spots by becoming emotionally involved. To counteract this, a team of therapists observes the session through a one-way mirror. These outside, neutral observers can see the entire picture and occasionally stop the session to provide the active therapists with fresh, broader points of view.

The Irreversibility of Seeing

Every act of learning can be conceptualized as an act of eye-opening. Learners see facts and connections they did not see earlier, they look at things from a new perspective. Just as cognitive learning may be a one-trial affair, or a continuing process, insights are sometimes gained suddenly, and sometimes are achieved gradually, by going through stages of therapy or self-analysis. However, once arrived at, unseeing is difficult if not impossible. Once the process of seeing begins – at either the individual or the family level – the process is irreversible. Seers, though sometimes temporarily regressing, cannot return to the protected position held earlier. They are in conflict, because having seen, they now must act, or be continually frustrated. Hannah Green's (1964) description of a 16-year-old schizophrenic adolescent provides a fitting ending to this chapter on blindness: "She had opened her mind to the words the way an eye used to darkness, veiled with its lashes, opens cautiously to the light, and, finding it even a little blinding, closes itself too late. The light had come, and come invincibly, even after the eye had renounced it. It was too late to unsee" (p. 72). Recovery then came slowly, not unopposed: "Deborah kept flying away to Yr's darkness, dissembling, and throwing up dust to hide in. She longed for blindness and ignorance, for now she realized that if she herself saw or recognized anything, it would have to be exposed for discussion, however shameful, fearful, or ugly it might be" (p. 127).

Activities

1 Pin the tail

Trigger: Each family member jots down 3 traits that s/he finds in the others, and attaches the small notes to their back, so they cannot see them. The traits chosen should affect the writer, with at least one being disturbing.

During the ensuing discussion with the therapist everyone says what s/he thinks each other family member thought of him/her, and why. They are then all confronted with what they think others think of them and what the others indeed wrote.

Possible point for discussion:

What do I feel about my hits and my misses?

2 Blind walk

Trigger: One person takes on the role of the blind (and is blindfolded), while another will be his/her guide who helps the blind person cross the room.

They leave the room, and the rest are instructed to interfere with them when they return. They can move the furniture to create obstacles, make noise, stand in their way. The therapist lends a hand. Repeat this either by another two persons or by switching their roles.

Possible points for discussion:

Talk about the kind of help one is comfortable or uncomfortable with, about
    needed vs. unneeded help, about sensitivity to the other's needs.
Do I know how to ask for help?
Do help and support make me feel good or angry? Where did I learn these
    responses?
How do I cope with obstacles in the family?

3 Blind spots

Trigger: Make a list of the things people say about you and you're sure they are dead wrong. Check with each person whether s/he wants to share this list with the rest of the family.

Once lists are ready:

What makes you feel they are wrong?
What makes them think that what they say about you is true?
How can you use your family members to understand this gap between
    what you think about yourself and what others think of you?
Discuss the process.

4 Train ride

Trigger: This is a guided imagination activity. Darken the room, speak slowly, in a relaxed, low voice: Sit in a comfortable position, close your eyes, breathe deeply. You're on a train. The train stops at a station where you felt safe, happy, satisfied with yourself. What made you feel so? Who was there? [pause] The train moves on to a station where you felt uncomfortable, embarrassed, unsure of yourself. Look around: What and whom do you see? [pause] You next stop in a dark tunnel. Here you felt bad about yourself, a failure. Who is at this station? What made you feel this way? [pause] At each station there were many people and factors. Move them aside and look only at yourself. What is it in you that brings about the best and the worst feelings and behaviors? [pause] Breathe deeply, move your limbs, open your eyes slowly. Turn on the lights.

Now you're with your family. Talk with them about these parts of you that bring out positive and negative feelings.

5 Picture gallery

Trigger: Give each family member a page with the outline of several picture frames drawn on it; label each with the name of a family member. Each of these pictures is a member of this family. Write on each a trait this person likes about him/herself, but isn't talked about in the family, and another trait this person dislikes, and is also left unspoken [e.g. dedicated mother likes to be in control; sis is a good student but hates being overweight]. Choose which of these are you willing to reveal to the others, so as to reduce "family blindness".

Possible points for discussion:

What do you gain and what do you lose by not talking about these things?
Is it easier to expose your own "blind" traits or those of others?
Is there a person here about whom the others tend to talk too much or too
    little?

6 To see ourselves as others see us

Trigger: This is a guided imagination activity. Darken the room, speak slowly, in a relaxed, low voice: Sit in a comfortable position, close your eyes, breathe deeply. Find a comfortable place, where you like to spend time at home. A family member enters, gives you feedback about something in you that disturbs him or her, and leaves. [Pause] Breathe deeply, move your limbs, open your eyes slowly. Turn on the lights.

Possible points for discussion:

What was s/he talking about?
Do I dare to find out?
What enables me to listen to feedback, and what makes me become
    resistant?

2

Distortions, or It's All for the Best!

She saw him pretending now nearly all the time, so as to avoid the clashes that had taken place almost weekly after the first six months of the marriage. Every time he opened his mouth she could hear that he did not mean a single word, but was trying only to disarm her by saying what he thought she wanted him to say. He would do anything now to avoid a battle, anything but really change. (Roth, 1968, p. 218)

Destructive Myths in Family Therapy: How to Overcome Barriers to Communication by Seeing and Saying – A Humanistic Perspective, First Edition. Daniela Kramer-Moore and Michael Moore.
© 2012 John Wiley & Sons, Ltd. Published 2012 by John Wiley & Sons, Ltd.

Poor eyesight prevents a person from obtaining a clear picture of reality. The analogy to our metaphorical seeing is obvious: various degrees of psychological blindness lead to a more or less distorted view of one's social environment. The importance of realistically reading one's surroundings is tremendous; considerable distortions (such as a deficit in insight, cognitive impairment, or the misinterpretation of perceptions or of experiences) are among the criteria for numerous individual and mental family disorders (American Psychiatric Association, 2000). In this chapter we shall examine several distortions, focusing on the toll they take on family well-being. Before we delve into the distortions that influence the life of groups, it will be helpful to examine their more basic form, namely individual or *ego defense mechanisms*. It should be noted that while we find the psychoanalytic approach underlying the theory of defense mechanisms very useful, it has not been universally accepted.

Freudian psychodynamic theory describes three structures of personality: the Id, the Ego and the Superego. Innate Id instincts demand immediate gratification; Superego or the moral authority of personality requires that such gratification either occurs according to socially accepted norms or be denied. It is the Ego's difficult task to bridge between these two conflicting dictates, along with negotiating environmental demands. When the Ego senses that it is in danger of losing control over either of the two other structures, it experiences anxiety. Freud (1959) considered anxiety a healthy warning signal that urges the Ego to take action; however it can become so overwhelming that the Ego resorts to extreme, irrational measures; these are the *ego defense mechanisms*. The latter have some common characteristics:

- The entire process of intrapsychic conflict, the resultant anxiety and its reduction through ego defense mechanisms occur in the unconscious region of personality. An individual is aware of the physiological and psychological symptoms of anxiety, but remains unconscious both of its causes and of the means the Ego uses for its alleviation.
- The short-term benefits gained by the reduction of the often extreme, even debilitating effects of anxiety come at a price: defense mechanisms distort reality which is rearranged, so that intra-psychic balance can be temporarily restored. Yet the conflict remains unresolved; instead of attending to it, the individual must now invest much needed energy in subterfuge.

A Few Ego Defense Mechanisms

Freud's original list of ego defense mechanisms has been extended throughout the years. Following are some of the most important and frequently encountered.

- *Repression*, or unconscious, motivated forgetting, may well serve as the basis for all the rest of the defenses. The distortion of reality in repression is simple and effective: it makes some offending thought or memory inaccessible. We literally forget that we did, said, or thought something forbidden by our moral sense: *I can't remember ever having said that, I didn't see it, I didn't do it!* This forgetting is an active process; repression has to be continually exerted to prevent the taboo material from reaching consciousness. It is necessary to add that the "reality" being distorted by this and other defense mechanisms is itself subject to interpretation and should not be regarded as having an objective, fixed status.
- *Rationalization* (quite similar to what social psychologists call the reduction of cognitive dissonance) involves the "explaining away" of some troublesome content. Any failure, and especially a failed relationship, is likely to cause anxiety, so how about rearranging reality: *the circumstances were wrong, I didn't get the support I needed, it was doomed to fail from the beginning*.
- In *projection* individuals attribute their own upsetting thoughts or unacceptable traits to another person: *I hate you. It's bad to hate, so I'd rather believe that it is you who hate me*. Projective personality tests, such as the Rorschach inkblots, the Thematic Apperception Test (or TAT), and Draw-A-Man type tasks, are all based on our predilection to project our hidden emotions and thoughts. By presenting test-takers with ambiguous, unstructured stimuli and tasks, these tests are designed to provide a convenient outlet for such secreted contents. (It must be mentioned that the validity of projective tests is severely contested.)
- *Displacement* channels one's objectionable emotions from their original target to a more acceptable one. Anger often gets mishandled this way, when one directs it at either the first available object or at a less threatening one than at the one who caused it (scapegoating is a similar process). Comparable dynamics may take place with respect to sexual urges as well: if the desired object is unreachable or unacceptable, the impulse may be redirected toward other objects or activities. As in all the

other cases, the displacing individual is unaware both of the distortion of reality taking place, and of the long-term damage caused by it.

- By using *Reaction Formation* an individual copes with an unacceptable emotion through expressing its opposite. When love toward someone is morally or culturally forbidden, hate may take its place; similarly, intense dislike may be replaced by outbursts of affection. Extremely held attitudes or entire ideologies (political, sexual, religious) are always suspect of covering their very opposite: This exaggeration protects one from even being close to holding a favorable attitude toward some emotionally laden, conflictful issue (such as homophobia and homosexuality, censorship and pornography, or religiosity and atheism).

Family Defense Mechanisms

The above are among the many ego defense mechanisms that serve individuals to ease their immediate discomfort, resulting from intrapsychic conflict. When members of tight-knit groups, such as the family, are faced with interpersonal conflicts, they use additional defenses that serve the entire system. We shall refer to these as Family Defense Mechanisms. Their list is even less well defined and rigid than that of the ones based on Freudian psychodynamic principles. The common thread running through all of them is again one of distortion. In order to avoid confronting difficulties which are anxiety producing and threatening the family unit's supposedly harmonious existence, an honest picture of "reality" is disregarded. Though they permit some sort of day-to-day functioning, a family's defense mechanisms make unresolved conflicts more and more difficult to solve. In many cases, the symptom-bearing member (IP) disturbs the family equilibrium, and is sacrificed by the others in their attempts to defend themselves. Distorting reality is dangerous not only for the current generation. Similarly to other PFPs, children learn these practices, regard them as normative and desirable, and carry them on to their future relationships. Eric Berne, the father of Transactional Analysis (1980, p. 103), used the picturesque expression "intensive field course" to describe such transgenerational transfer, in which children learn the behavioral patterns or games their parents play.

"Blurred vision" occurs outside the family, as well. Distortion of reality takes place in cohesive groups, where under certain conditions "groupthink" is likely to develop, and may involve such symptoms as illusions of invulnerability, stereotyping of opponents, illusions of unanimity and so forth. (For recent work on groupthink see Turner, Pratkanis, and Struckman, 2007).

Homeostasis (the subject of Chapter 5) refers to the tendency of systems to maintain equilibrium by resisting change, and to restore equilibrium when some unavoidable change occurs. In families the homeostatic motive guarantees a stable, secure existence, according to well-known rules. Yet, at the same time it is pathogenic to some extent, since it prevents development and responsiveness to the constantly changing needs of family members. Behaving towards toddlers as if they were still infants, toward adolescents as to 10-year-olds, or toward young adults as to adolescents are commonly seen examples of such homeostatic responses. The rigidity of a family becomes especially apparent in times of conflicts and crises, when they employ behavior patterns that are doomed to fail. For example, the domineering parent will exercise excessive control over the rebellious adolescent; that is to say, s/he will use the very pathological family process that made the adolescent rebel in the first place. When nagging spouses sense that their partner needs distance, they react by increased nagging. For a clinical example of this, as well as the following family defense mechanisms, see Box 2.1.

Box 2.1 Brief examples of family defense mechanisms drawn from clinical practice

By its nature a practice in family therapy is an inexhaustible source of real life illustrations of the distortions mentioned in this chapter. While all of the following vignettes are based on actual cases, some demographic characteristics have been changed to protect the clients and their families. These cases have been selected to best illustrate a specific family defense mechanism. This does not preclude the possibility of some unavoidable overlaps: homeostatic cases often contain enmeshment; codependency has homeostatic ingredients; both fusion and triangulation may lead to emotional cut-off, and so forth.

Homeostasis – in this family doors inside the home have never been closed, not even when the children became adolescents. When the teenager daughter brings home some friends and wants to close the door of her room, the mother demands of the therapist to explain to

(*continued*)

her daughter that in good families there are no secrets. The daughter's need for privacy is regarded as an act of betrayal.

Disengagement – the 6-year-old son of career oriented parents is not picked up after school, and he cannot say where his parents are. A teacher again stays with him until evening, when his mother realizes that he is not at home. The two older boys (10 and 12) of this family are latchkey children.

Enmeshment – this mother's married daughter is studying abroad. The mother arranges for (and the daughter readily assents to) a 24-hour link on Skype, which provides her with constant audio-visual connection into the daughter's household. In a therapy session (initiated by another daughter who feels neglected) the mother is proud of her strong connection to her daughter and grandchildren as the ultimate demonstration of the family's closeness.

Pseudo-mutuality – in this "perfect" family, holidays, birthdays, and other important events are celebrated with lavish parties; snapshots of smiling family members are carefully kept in albums and shown to guests. Therapy sessions reveal that there is no intimacy between spouses, between parents and children or between siblings. They know nothing about each others' inner world. Each of the parents asks for an individual session, unwilling to open themselves to the therapist in the presence of others. They all feel isolated, yet they are already planning their next picnic.

Codependency – a 36-year-old widowed business woman, mother of two boys, marries a concert pianist and gives up everything – business, further education, care of her children – to cater to him. In so doing she replaces his previous codependency as the socially and emotionally dysfunctional only son of a mother who took care of all his needs, while he devoted himself entirely to music.

Triangulation – every time there is conflict between the parents of two teenagers (a boy and a girl), the mother enlists the son to support her. This recurrent pattern ends with the father cutting himself off (see below). His place is taken by the daughter, with her mother demanding the son's intervention in the bitter mother–daughter conflicts, leading to a cutting off on the daughter's part.

(*continued*)

Secrets and taboos – the 15-year-old daughter of two highly-educated parents suffers from epileptic attacks. Her condition is kept as a secret outside the immediate family. When her school mates witness an attack and confront her, she denies that she is ill. Her fear of revealing her secret keeps her distant from her peers

Cutting of – the 20-year-old daughter of a domineering mother and an emotionally absent father distances herself from her wealthy parents by moving to another continent, changing her religion, and marrying an ultraorthodox Jew. Her breakout is unsuccessful: After a few years she submits to her parents' emotional and financial pressure, divorces and returns to her family of origin, thus cutting herself and her young child off from her husband. She lives with her parents, giving them total control over her child.

Fusion – the adolescent son of a divorced couple (enmeshing mother, disengaged father, older sister has cut herself off) refuses to communicate with his father. He is unable to either separate the cognitive from the emotional aspects of his parents' conflict, or to regard himself as an entity separate in opinions or emotions from those of his mother. Having been sucked into and taken sides in the marital conflict, he has lost contact with the only significant male figure in his life.

Double binding– the parents of this 23-year-old woman unceasingly urge her to marry, yet they frustrate all her efforts by finding fault with every single boyfriend she brings home. The consequences of double-binding include her hasty marriage to and eventual divorce from one of the more unsuitable (in her parents' continually expressed opinion) partners. She is again without a partner, taking care of her elderly parents, who keep pushing her to find a man who is up to their standards.

Complementary relationship – on the first day of their marriage she told him that the kitchen and the children were her territory. Twelve years, five children, and a master's degree later, she cannot cope with the stress she is under, yet her husband is unwilling to make any change: he is happy with the division of labor and the clear boundaries, continuously reminding her that this was her choice.

Symmetrical relationship – this couple is in a perpetual contest (which they try to bring into the therapy session, as well) about whose

(*continued*)

life is more difficult. They quarrel practically every evening: he works long hours; she takes care of the house and the children in addition to her part-time job. He claims she neither earns nor cleans enough; she complains about his not lending a hand with household chores.

Enmeshment – in enmeshed families "members are over-concerned and over-involved in each other's lives. In extreme cases, the family's lack of differentiation between subsystems makes separation from the family an act of betrayal" (Goldenberg and Goldenberg, 2008, p. 244). Psychological boundaries between enmeshed family members are weak and permeable to such an extent that they seem to live each other's lives. Though individuals in such a family may overtly justify their over-involvement ("She needs me"; "we are like two peas in a pod!"), they also experience ambivalence, frustration and anger, for the need to free themselves gnaws at them incessantly. The immediate gains one receives from enmeshment (such as being assisted in coping) are offset by both the long-term loss of autonomy, and individuals' difficulty to create intimate ties with people outside the family. It is not necessary for the entire family to participate in this pathological process; in family therapy parent–child enmeshments are often observed, and are likely to be related to a spouse's need to escape a disappointing marital relationship.

Disengagement – enmeshment and disengagement may be regarded as two extremes on a continuum. While in the former family members' freedom is restricted by the constant and excessive concern of others, in the latter they are isolated from each other, with each person living in his or her private bubble. Boundaries between individuals are so strong that they refrain from asking for or offering help to each other. Minuchin (1974) found that such "inappropriately rigid boundaries" made communication within the family difficult and handicapped the protective functions of the family. Children growing up in such a family will learn not to put their trust in others. In contrast to enmeshed families' total commitment to a "one for all and all for one" policy, members of a disengaged family may lack all sense of family loyalty.

Pseudo-mutuality – coined by the psychiatrist and family therapist Lyman Wynne in the 1950s, this family defense mechanism was recently defined as "an atmosphere maintained by family members in which surface harmony and a high degree of agreement with one another hide deep and destructive intrapsychic and interpersonal conflicts. The family acts 'as if' it is close and happy when in fact it is not" (Anderson et al., 2009). This façade of harmony is kept up by family members (often by strict adherence to rites and rituals) so as to avoid open conflict and possible break-up of the unit, and is often accompanied by proclamations of "We are such a good family!" Any attempt to alter this extremely powerful family myth by a dissenting member (most likely the IP) is guilt-producing and attacked by the rest of the family. The family's insistence on unity prevents individuals from developing their own sense of self-identity.

Codependency first described the sometimes dysfunctional relationship between an alcoholic and a family member, but is currently used to characterize other conditions in which there is an "unhealthy devotion to a relationship at the cost of one's personal and psychological needs" (Springer, Britt, and Schlenker, 1998). This process is nearly synonymous with the still older term of *Interlocking Pathology* (reviewed by Goldenberg and Goldenberg, 2008, p. 158); both refer to situations in which (usually) two individuals cater to each other's complementary and pathological needs: the devoted codependent needs the physically or emotionally disabled other to raise his or her self-esteem, while the latter has secondary gains from being taken care of. There is an obvious homeostatic component to this process, for it is in either one or both participants' interest to maintain the codependent relationship. Attempts at breaking up the dysfunctional bond either by one of the participants or by outsiders are therefore robustly resisted. As with many other family defenses, the roots of codependency can be found in one's family of origin: Reyome and Ward (2007) reported significant correlations between scores on a codependency scale and reports of emotional neglect, emotional abuse and physical abuse in childhood.

Triangulation – Bowen (1976a) introduced this term to describe what dyads (two-person groups) tend to do in times of tension and anxiety: they draw in a third person and so shift attention from themselves to other parts of the system. Nichols and Schwartz (2006, p. 450) described this maneuver as "Detouring conflict between two people by involving a third person, stabilizing the relationship between the original pair." Often the triangulated person is less powerful than the members of the original dyad. In families it is the children who are most vulnerable, and are often drawn into the conflict between their parents. There are many ways in which this move can then develop: the child may develop behavioral problems, thus deflecting attention from the parental problem, or it may use its position to play the parents off against each other. It is also possible for one of the parents to form a coalition with the child against the other parent. A basic characteristic of all defense mechanisms is apparent here: instead of solving a conflict, the participants resort to a measure which gives some temporary relief, but eventually results in added distress.

Secrets and taboos – restrictions of communication within a social system are, by definition, symptoms of pathology. Rogers (1967) attributed to this issue utmost importance: "The whole task of psychotherapy is the task of dealing with a failure in communication . . . Good communication, free communication, within or between men, is always therapeutic" (p. 330). Forbidden topics and secrets are prime examples of the family as a whole, or a subsystem within the family, attempting to manage the flow of information. Whether this is done out of a need for control, or in order to avoid the unpleasantness of dealing with painful and embarrassing topics, results are the same: issues that require the most airing and subsequent resolution, receive the least attention. (More on the suppression of communication within the family appears under "Let's not talk about it" in Chapter 5).

Fusion – one of the most basic forms of distortion occurs when individuals' emotions severely interfere with their ability to perceive and cognitively process reality. The degree to which individuals *fuse* cognition and affect, also referred to as a lack of differentiation of the self, is a core concept in Bowen's (1976a) family systems theory. Goldenberg and Goldenberg (2008, p. 468) defined it as "the merging of the intellectual and emotional aspects of a family member, paralleling the degree to which that person is caught up in, and loses a separate sense of self in, family relationships." Bowen found that those who fail to differentiate between these two aspects exhibit poor functioning within their family and are rigid and unable to adapt to changing situations. When starting a relationship, men and women tend to seek out partners who are similar to themselves in their degree of differentiation. This leads to serious complications when two persons with a high degree of fusion marry: poor functioning, anxiety, emotional distancing (see also Bowen's related concepts of solid self and pseudo self in Chapter 6).

Cutting off – to escape from an unresolved emotional attachment to their parents, individuals may distance themselves either by emotional isolation or by physically running away. Bowen (1976a) theorized that the more intense such cut-off with their past, the more likely are persons to bring this emotional reaction to their marriage, and the more likely their children will be to cut themselves off. Emotionally cut-off adults have a fear of intimacy and often present a strong façade of independence. Several scales have been developed to measure various aspects of Bowen's theory. McCollum's (1991) Emotional Cut-off Scale, for instance, includes such items as "I have contact with my mother more out of a sense of enjoyment than out of a sense of obligation." Using another set of items for the measurement of this variable, Peleg (2008) found that marital satisfaction was indeed negatively correlated with a person's emotional cut-off score: those who appeared aloof and isolated from others, denied the importance of the family, or often boasted of their own emancipation from their parents, were less satisfied with their marriage than persons with low scores on the cut-off scale.

Double-binding – "The essential hypothesis of the double bind theory is that the 'victim' – the person who becomes psychotically unwell – finds him or herself in a communicational matrix, in which messages contradict each other, the contradiction is not able to be communicated on and the unwell person is not able to leave the field of interaction." This is how Gibney (2006) summarized Gregory Bateson's famous theory, connecting certain "damned if you do, damned if you don't"-type communication patterns within families with the development of schizophrenia. Contradictory demands are confusing and frustrating under any circumstance; they are particularly dangerous when frequently issued by a person of authority. A father may, for instance, demand more independence from his adolescent son, who by obeying him would show lack of independence. Or consider the situation of the daughter, whose mother first criticizes her for being shy, then berates her for "wearing her heart on her sleeve." If either of these youths try to point out the inconsistency of the demand, they are likely to be told "not to talk back." Since they are likely to lack the means or the strength to separate themselves from their double-binding parents, they are also prevented from "leaving the field." While currently there is some doubt about the acceptability of the above hypothesis (that is to say, whether contradictory messages contribute to the development of some psychoses), Gibney (2006) concluded his review of the half-century-old double-bind theory by recalling his clinical observations, where "it can be startlingly witnessed that in some families, double binds in communication are still crazy-making, after all these years." Without specifically implicating communication problems, several recent studies have found a relationship between childhood trauma (both physical and emotional) and psychotic symptoms (e.g. Arseneault et al., 2011).

Why do some people engage in double-binding? A likely mechanism for acquiring this dangerous habit is transgenerational transmission. Without a conscious and persistent effort to change a behavior one has seen again and again in childhood, it will reappear in adulthood (see pp. 2–3), indeed, it will seem as the only appropriate response. This is especially the case in stressful, anxiety provoking situations, where *fusion* prevents one from "counting to twenty."

Complementary, symmetrical, and parallel relationships – the description of non-egalitarian relationships by Lederer and Jackson (1968) as either *complementary* or *symmetrical* is also related to distortion. In complementary marriages there seems to be an unwritten contract between the spouses, providing for the traits and activities of one to complement those missing in the other. Rather than being an ideal structure, once this type of relationship evolves, its stereotyped, hierarchical nature leaves no freedom for the participants to act naturally. Their need to keep clear boundaries and so to avoid conflicts comes at a price: the participants' self is diminished by being excluded from large parts of family life. Distortions are likely to take place in both of them, with each person rendering the other's behavior more extreme. In order to avoid open conflict a wife, for example, may hide her talents, so that her husband may shine brighter. Similarly, a husband may force himself to show lack of interest in various activities (regarding children, housekeeping, or gardening) and declare them as the wife's territory. When one spouse is dominant, forceful, and vociferous, the other one becomes submissive, weak and silent. A pathogenic version of the complementary structure is the *marital skew* (originally proposed by Lidz, Flack, and Cornelison, 1965). The basis of such a relationship is a spouse who is seriously disturbed, and one who is weak and dependent. The former dominates the system, while the latter pretends to self, the children and the outside world that the family is normal. Through the distortion and denial of reality a severe PFP is thus accepted as normal. This is a destructive yet stable system, which might act as the breeding ground for a schizophrenic offspring (see also *codependency*, above).

Distortion is also present in symmetrical marriages. These are basically competitive relationships, where each spouse's anxiety over the lack of self-value leads him/her to be engaged in a constant combat to prove superiority over the other in relation to their similar abilities and activities. The one-upmanship they practice prevents them from acting as a team; their relationship can become dysfunctional due to the amount of energy wasted on rivalry. In their day-to-day interaction participants in a symmetrical dyad may constantly try to prove each other wrong, fight over the right to speak, or attempt to outdo one another in some trivial activity. The most extreme version of symmetry, described by Lidz, Flack, and Cornelison (1965), is the *marital schism*, in which two spouses compete for the love and support of their children by undermining each other's worth.

Before continuing, we must emphasize that there is nothing inherently wrong with either occasional competition or the balancing of one's abilities with someone else's. Both of these behavior patterns will now and then occur as elements of healthy, *parallel* partnerships, which are based on equality. The difference we observe here between rigid vs. flexible roles is not limited to problems that arise in complementary and symmetrical relationships (cf. Bowen, 1976a, re the healthy alternation of the dominant vs. adaptive roles in marriage). Just think of a family's clown, who has to entertain his or her circle regardless of circumstances, or of the scapegoat, who is always blamed for whatever goes wrong. Such rigid adherence to roles always interferes with the family's problem-solving ability, and must by necessity distort their holders' perception of reality. (We will have more to say about roles in Chapter 3).

This chapter has dealt with the many ways vision of individuals and families is obscured and distorted. In conclusion, let us ask ourselves: Why is seeing so dangerous, why is so strong a defense erected against it? We find that its irreversibility has much to do with the threat it presents: once their vision becomes clear, seers cannot return to their previously held protected position. This breakdown of homeostasis – against which distortive defenses are used – is the necessary starting point of therapy.

Activities

1 Family map 1

Trigger: Each person draws a map that represents the family, with each member being a continent (or an island). Reassure them that they may but will not have to show this map to anyone. The continents have different shapes, sizes, contours, locations relative to each other, representing each member's position in the family.

Look at your map: What do you feel? What would you like to change? What needs to happen for such a change? [e.g. change size, become more or less central, accessible, etc.]. When the maps are folded and put away, talk about the process.

If the maps were not revealed:

What needs to happen in this family for you to feel comfortable about showing your map?

What have you learned about yourself in this meeting?
What have you learned about your family?

2 Family map 2

This is a variation of the previous activity.

Trigger: Let the clients know that the maps they draw will be shared with their family: We'll look at the possibly different perceptions you have of your family. There are no right or wrong pictures of the family, only legitimately subjective perceptions. When these perceptions differ a lot, there may be some pain that needs to be talked about. Place the maps in the middle of the circle and look at the different perceptions.

Possible points for discussion:

How do you feel about what you see?
What are the important differences between the maps?
What would you like to change?
Look at the other maps. Are you happy with your place there?

3 Family gossip

Trigger: One of the family members turns his/her back to the group and the rest gossip about him/her. S/he then faces the group and says, without trying to justify or defend self, what s/he felt and thought while hearing this gossiping.

Possible points for discussion:

Was there anything new learned?
Have they missed anything important?

Therapist intervenes, redirects if necessary, and may repeat with other members.

This activity can be repeated throughout the course of therapy to see whether openness and authenticity have increased, along with the ability of the family to cope.

4 *What do the neighbors think about us?*

This activity can be used to introduce pseudo-mutuality issues.

Trigger: How would your neighbors describe your family, your marriage, your children? Turn what they see into a "family snapshot." Stand up and create the scene your neighbors see. When this is done: If the onlookers gave each of you a sentence that best describes you, what would it be?

Then: Does the neighbors' picture of this family differ from yours? In what way?

Discuss the differences.

Now each of you, in his or her turn, get out of the picture [therapist takes their place, assuming same pose] and look at it. How does it relate to your perception of the family? Is something missing? Is this the way you want to be seen? Is there something you'd rather not show to outsiders? Ask one of the family to create a picture of the family at one of its painful moments. What do you say to this picture? What do you feel? What's needed to face this picture and to talk about the pain?

Reflect on what has happened.

5 *Masquerade*

Trigger: Give each participant a folded page. Ask each to draw (or describe in words) on the exposed half of the page the mask they feel is worn by each family member (including self). Then on the inner half of the page (that falls immediately below the first) ask them to draw or describe what they think lies behind the mask.

Ask them to reflect:

Relate to the difference between the overt and the covert selves.
What are the gains and losses of wearing a mask?
What has to happen for family members to unmask?

Ask each person to reflect upon what was discovered during this activity.

3

Insight through Therapy, or To See or Not To See

I shut my eyes in order to see. (Attributed to Paul Gauguin)

In the vast and varied field of psychotherapies (at the time of writing, Wikipedia's list was 161 long) Family Therapy belongs to those committed to an inter-, rather than intrapersonal perspective. While many of the principles and techniques of individual therapy can be applied to both small groups and families, this shift toward exploring the interaction between individuals and utilizing the information that is gained there, is the essence of family therapy. Predictably, there are variations within this field, mainly due to their major proponents' original identification (and subsequent dissatisfaction) with another psychotherapy. Some of the best known family therapies, along with the name of their major figures, are:

Destructive Myths in Family Therapy: How to Overcome Barriers to Communication by Seeing and Saying – A Humanistic Perspective, First Edition. Daniela Kramer-Moore and Michael Moore.
© 2012 John Wiley & Sons, Ltd. Published 2012 by John Wiley & Sons, Ltd.

Transgenerational (Murray Bowen);
Experiential (Carl Whitaker);
Psychodynamic (Nathan Ackerman);
Conjoint (Virginia Satir);
Strategic (John Weakland and Paul Watzlawick);
Structural (Salvador Minuchin);
Milan Systemic (Selvini Palazzoli);
Contextual (Ivan Boszormenyi-Nagy);
Cognitive behavioral (Aaron Beck);
Social constructionist (Michael White);
Behavioral (Ian Falloon);
Person-centered (Ned Gaylin).

This vaguely chronological list is neither exhaustive nor exclusive. On the one hand, many others have greatly contributed to the field; on the other hand, there are considerable overlaps among the various schools. Instead of dwelling on the nature of these therapies (well described in several recently published overviews: see Becvar and Becvar, 2009; Carr, 2006; Goldenberg and Goldenberg, 2008; Nichols, 2009), we identify with Yalom, who advocates the creation of a new therapy for every client (Yalom, 1997, p. 221). One of his fictional alter egos proclaims: "My technique is to abandon technique. My technique is to tell the truth" (Yalom, 1997, p. 43). This approach to a large extent overlaps with the stance taken by Rogers (e.g. 1990a), as pointed out by Brazier (1997): "If we follow what he [Rogers] said, we are not following what he said, because what he said was that we should find our own way." This stipulation of course concerns techniques of therapy more than it does basic attitudes: Rogers repeatedly emphasized that congruence, unconditional positive regard, empathy (see Box 3.1), and respect are the vital ingredients of any good therapy, rather than concrete recipes and formulas of intervention (Lietaer, 1997).

Box 3.1 The role of empathy

Empathy, that is, the ability to put oneself emotionally in the place of another, has a particular importance in any type of psychotherapy. It plays a double role in the therapeutic process: It is both a means and

(*continued*)

a goal. In its first role, Rogers (1990b, pp. 226–227; Kramer-Moore and Moore, 2005, p. 124) suggested that empathy on the part of the therapist is one of the necessary and sufficient conditions of therapeutic personality change. Unless the client's world is clear to the therapist, there can be no effective communication between them. While representing a therapeutic approach quite different from Rogerian humanism, the psychoanalyst Heinz Kohut agreed: "Empathy is a mode of cognition which is specifically attuned to the perception of complex psychological configurations . . . Replacement of empathy . . . by other modes of observation leads to a mechanistic and lifeless conception of psychological reality" (1971, pp. 300–301).

Empathy's second role concerns the outcome of therapy. It is not enough for therapists to be able to put themselves in their clients' shoes, as it were; Kohut regarded empathy (along with humor, wisdom, and creativeness), as one of the new complex personality structures that result from successful therapy (1971, p. 199). This is achieved both directly and indirectly: the therapist encourages empathic communications and draws attention to non-empathic ones; s/he also provides a model for empathic communicating and listening.

How important is empathy? The influential American philosopher, sociologist and psychologist George Herbert Mead (1934, p. 141) equated the ability to put oneself in the place of others as the very essence of human intelligence. Kohut (1978, p. 705) found that empathy is the "psychological nutrient without which human life . . . could not be sustained." In the context of counselor education, Kaffenberger, Gibb, and Murphy (2002) concluded that the use of empathy may have been a cornerstone of the skills they hoped to impart to their students, the most central skill they taught: "Empathy is not so much a specific skill taught in group process as it is the clay that allows groups to form" (p. 105).

The Goals of Therapy

Some of the goals of therapy are applicable to every family, while others fit the specific needs of the family at hand. We will presently have something to say about the former. As for the latter: the needs of the family in therapy are first stated during the *mapping of family pain* (see below), then they are revisited and probably changed during the forthcoming sessions, and they again surface at the closing of therapy, when their level of attainment is evaluated.

The general goal of therapy is the reduction of family pain. By the time they arrive for their first session, some members of the family have been in pain for a considerable time. The family, as a unit, may have been functional (parents working, children studying, breakfast on the table), with one or more of them silently suffering, and then signaling the need for either individual or family therapy. In other apparently functional families, there is an IP who is responsible for the parents' presence: "We're fine; s/he is our only problem!" And then there are clearly dysfunctional family units, where the pain caused by day-to-day difficulties is both severe and undisguised. In all of these situations the reduction of pain is not only curative but also preventative, for whatever the current status is, it is likely to become worse if left unattended. "Let's not talk about it!" and similar sayings (to be discussed in Chapter 5) are not the cure but rather the core of family pain. We must point out that the reduction of pain is a long-term goal: The process itself – gaining insight, experiencing change – can be very painful, and has to be accompanied by the therapist's empathic support.

Another general goal has to do with the question of the preservation of marriage. We do not a priori regard the family as sacred, or the keeping together of the family at any cost as the ultimate goal of therapy. If the couple agree that the perpetuation of the marriage is their goal, then the family therapist assists them in achieving it, to his or her best ability. In other cases it becomes clear quite early in therapy that while a couple may cling to a myth concerning the durability of marriage, they share very little and dislike each other. By helping them to abandon the myth and to peacefully separate, the family therapist also enables their children to keep a healthy contact with their divorced parents, without becoming victims of these parents' overt and covert anger. Other complications arise in the frequent case of one spouse asking to end the marriage, with the other one trying to hold on to it. Here the family therapist can help them gain insight into the gains and losses of each alternative to all family members.

A further important therapeutic goal, applicable to every family, is the acquiring of congruent communication skills (to be discussed in detail in Chapter 6). Incongruence and the lack of authenticity are likely to lie at the bottom of many family problems. During therapy the family learns both through observing the therapist's communication pattern and by the latter's drawing attention to lapses and hidden agendas that each member can express his or her needs and emotions freely, without censorship (see relevant portions of "Agreement" in Chapter 4).

Stages of Therapy

Individuals and families, once aware of the urgent need to change something in their behavior, may attempt to deal with their symptoms. Thus, an abusive husband may decide to stop being aggressive toward his wife, or a truant teenager may promise not to break the rules anymore. Even if they succeed for a while in suppressing their symptoms, the first-order change they have brought about is insufficient, for symptoms only mask some deep-rooted, systemic problem.

The goal of therapy is to bring about second-order changes, that is, changes in the structure and the functioning of the family system itself. In order to help a disabling family develop into an enabling one, focus must be shifted from the IP to the family system, and from the presenting problem to underlying dynamics. It is insufficient for just the therapist to see beyond Layer A; in order to minimize resistance, and promote second-order change, members of the family must become aware of the existence and the messages of Layers B and C, as well.

While there are no fast-and-hard rules about the exact sequence of events in therapy, it is possible to recognize three naturally occurring stages: the recognition of PFPs, the implementation of change, and the bringing of therapy to an end.

Stage 1: Insightful recognition of PFPs

The therapist's main goal during this stage is to promote seeing and relabeling of existing dynamics, thus assisting the family to overcome their paralyzing status quo (see "stopping and reflecting" in Chapter 1). Recognition requires the ability to observe oneself and others within the family context. Only when individuals accept responsibility for their share of the PFPs, will there be readiness to change, rather than the need to change others. Within this stage there is a growing awareness that the old homeostatic routine is dysfunctional, and that the IP is the family scapegoat and not the source of all their troubles. Becoming aware of, and understanding the family dynamics and each member's contribution to the family pain are vital steps toward change. We shall outline here the first three sessions of therapy, realizing that the subsequent ones depend not only on specific family themes and dynamics, but also on each family's characteristic rhythm.

In the first, introductory session, even compliant family members are likely to experience a lot of anxiety: they find themselves in an unfamiliar situation, where they are expected to open up to a stranger. Some of the participants expect to be vindicated, others are afraid of being accused and condemned by the therapist whom they regard as a referee. For the therapist, too, this is a tense occasion. During this session s/he has to size up each individual family member, as well as the coalitions among them, and to receive a first account of perceived goals (which are likely to change as therapy develops). S/he must come across as a trustworthy, neutral, non-judgmental, empathic listener, who is not going to give advice or directions. S/he is not to appear as an infallible expert, but rather as a professional who is willing to learn together with this family; a team member rather than an adversary. There are two important messages that each family member should take away from this meeting.

1. No one knows the family better than the family members themselves. The therapist's task is to help them clarify and compare the costs and benefits of their options, and to illuminate some processes to which they may be blind.
2. Everyone has a chance of gaining something from these sessions, so that the considerable investment of time, energy, and money will be justified.

When the stage is set and the appropriate climate for therapy is established, the second session can be devoted to the drawing up of a verbal *Agreement* (see Chapter 4 for details). This agreement is not the same as the often encountered contract between therapist and client, though the two may partially overlap. We are not talking of a contract as in the contractual method of Transactional Analysis, neither is this agreement a legal contract, such as suggested by Tudor (1999, pp. 221–222). Instead, it is a carefully negotiated working agreement, which makes it possible for family members to function in a relatively safe setting, and may be re-evaluated and redrawn according to changing needs. Negotiating the agreement is not a technical step but an integral part of the therapeutic process, for it enables members of the family to see both their own and their partners' needs, perhaps for the first time; it also serves as a model for creating family agreements in future family conflicts.

The third session is best described as *mapping family pain.* Its purpose is to obtain a baseline for the family and to develop the therapeutic process. Every member is asked to create his or her own view of the conflicts and the pains experienced by family members. In some families this is achieved with ease in an unstructured manner; for others there are various techniques of family mapping (preferably non-verbal, so that independent impressions can be obtained): molding Plasticine figurines, drawing stick figures, creating a map where countries stand for individuals, and so on. We have found *genograms* (a variation of the well-known family tree; see Box 3.2) to be especially useful.

Box 3.2 The genogram

A genogram (see McGoldrick, Gerson, and Shellenberger, 1999) is a graphical depiction of an individual's family connections. In addition to the links that appear in family trees, it also contains information about the strength and type of emotional ties between family members. The most often used symbols used in a genogram follow.

Circle: female (inscribe name and age; identify self by double lines).
Square: male (inscribe name and age; identify self by double lines).
Triangle: pregnancy (inscribe square or circle if fetus' gender is known).
X superimposed on the above: deceased.
Connecting line: marriage or offspring.
Slash across connection: divorce of spouse or cut-off of other relative.
Single line: regular emotional relationship.
Double line: strong emotional relationship.
Broken line: weak emotional relationship.
Wavy line: stormy emotional relationship.
Flag on connecting line: source of pain or conflict.

Add key and use colors to indicate positive and negative relationships and any other symbol to indicate love, friendship, enmity, etc.

In large families include only individuals who are meaningful to your narrative.

When the resultant family maps are compared, the gaps between different views of the family are often anxiety provoking; here is another opportunity for the therapist to encourage a pluralistic attitude by legitimizing subjective, possibly contradictory conceptions.

A possible ending of this third session is a request from each participant to create a map of their ideal family (see Activities 1 and 2 in Chapter 2), the one in which there is no pain or conflict. A verbal equivalent of this is the "magic wand" exercise, where each family member is asked how a family event (or the family map) would look like if they could all change by waving a magic wand. This activity can lead to the further identification of significant themes, such as the gap between expectations and reality, which need to be addressed in order to move forward.

Stage 2: The implementation of change

Stage 1 of the therapeutic process was mostly about seeing, but seeing is not enough, actions must follow, some change must occur. The implementation of change is made possible by helping the family to go through unlearning their PFPs and to adopt new attitudes and functional behavior patterns. Resistance to change often originates from an ignorance of alternative behaviors. The therapist functions as a teacher by offering healthier options and by providing opportunities to exercise them in a sheltered environment. The implementation of changes in the therapy session precedes their actualization in everyday life. Structural changes and the learning of communication skills go hand in hand: when members are able to communicate congruently with each other, the previously power driven family structure is likely to become more egalitarian.

During Stage 2 therapy sessions tend to focus on specific family themes. In spite of the vast differences among families, several common themes often crop up during therapy; to these we shall turn next.

Developing family themes: Coping with family stress   Family life has many stressful situations, creating symptoms that range from mild anxiety to depression. Bowen (1978, p. 472) found that individuals who have a low differentiation of self (that is to say, their thinking and feeling are fused) have an increased vulnerability to stress, and recover from stress-related symptoms slowly or not at all, while at the other end of the differentiation scale they tend to recover rapidly. Both Bowen (1978) and Satir (1988, p. 80) noticed that when under stress, people use dysfunctional, incongruent patterns of communication.

McGoldrick and Carter (2003) distinguished between horizontal and vertical stressors: while the former have to do with transitions in any family's life cycle, as well as with unpredictable, acute traumas, the latter derive from a given family's individual structure and dynamics, as well as from their myths, secrets and traditions. The two types of stressors interact: "The anxiety engendered on the vertical and horizontal axes when they converge, as well as the interaction of the various systems and how they work together to support or impede one another, are the key determinants of how well a family will manage its transitions through life" (McGoldrick and Carter, 2003, p. 381).

The distinction between horizontal and vertical stress is highly significant for the therapist. In acute, horizontal stress, the therapist's task is to help the family engage in teamwork, avoid turning against each other, develop better coping mechanisms, which may include finding community resources and support groups (see Galvin, Bylund, and Brommel, 2008, regarding the importance of communication for coping with the effects of stress). In more chronic, vertical stress, such as unhealthy roles, dysfunctional communication, or isolation of family members, the therapist can help them see what is happening, gain insight, reflect, set realistic goals, and initiate gradual changes in each of the stressful areas.

A family's style of dealing with stress is influenced by their position on a continuum ranging from enmeshment to disengagement. In highly enmeshed families the entire system is involved in solving an individual's problems. The opposite is true of disengaged families, where individual difficulties can go unnoticed until they become catastrophic. Minuchin (1974, pp. 54–56) pointed out that neither of these extreme responses is healthy; it is the therapist's task to act as a "boundary maker", by clarifying the obscure, often nonexistent boundaries typical of enmeshment and by loosening the overly rigid boundaries of disengaged family systems.

Developing family themes: Intimacy vs. control   Many families present themselves in therapy as loving, close-knit units whose only reason for needing help is a single, discordant member. The latter has a troubling symptom and needs to be cured: for example, depression, an eating disorder, reclusiveness, temper tantrums. It will not take long for the therapist to discover that what the family calls closeness, s/he calls enmeshment; their togetherness is based on a fear of disagreement; their love is synonymous with control. Family members' (often but not exclusively one of the parents') need to be needed requires constant reassurance; they cope with their anxiety over separation and their fear of becoming redundant by using others to validate themselves. This PFP is likely to have transgenerational aspects, with a similar pattern of emotional stuck-togetherness (Murray Bowen's term in his 1976a essay) present in both the previous and the next generations.

The exercise of control in these families occurs at the expense of healthy communication and intimacy. When it is one spouse who controls the other, both suffer: the controller finds him/herself in a relationship with a weakling who invites humiliation, while the controlled one goes through life without his or her voice being heard or needs and opinions being attended to. The former is unsatisfied because of not having met his or her equal; the latter becomes passive-aggressive, trying to take revenge indirectly. In our clinical experience extramarital affairs often have such a relationship at their background. Therapeutic intervention is resisted by the controller, who is afraid to lose power; the therapist needs to encourage the voiceless, controlled partner to provide some compensation, such as intimate communication, quality time, and affection. The stumbling block is the latter's accumulated anger and resentment, made more potent by a growing awareness of his or her inferior status. We have found it helpful not to make loud announcements about controller and controlled, but rather have the couple describe a conflictual scene from their marriage. They can then be shown how the unequal distribution of power affects their relationship: it may reduce anxiety in the short run, but it creates distance and coldness between the participants. The couple can be asked to change roles in order to empathize with the other's position, and to rewrite the scene in such a way that both participants' needs are respected (see I-messages on p. 75).

Unlike spousal relations, the parent–child nexus is inherently unequal: parents will always have more resources and be more powerful than their young children. Yet the style of parenting (discussed at more length in Chapter 7) makes all the difference: Authoritarian parents can limit their children's growth. Children's growing independence, their need to distance themselves from their parents and to join their peer group can be anxiety provoking. Instead of a healthy letting-go, controlling parents tighten their hold and resort to myths and rationalizations: "I don't want you to make the same mistakes I made"; "You're too young to know what's good for you"; "You'll thank me for this later." Whether they become obedient or rebellious, these children are prevented from making independent decisions – a vital step toward healthy maturation.

We have now seen the dangers of control. Yet a total lack of control is also problematic. In disengaged families the parents are uninvolved in their children's lives, totally occupied either as individuals or as a couple. These families are unlikely to be in therapy, and their children fend for themselves, for better or worse. Another type of lack of control characterizes parents who do not set boundaries for their children for fear of being rejected. Their parenting style is referred to as indulgent, permissive, or laissez-faire. Writing about the need to set boundaries without becoming authoritarian Dreikurs, Grunwald, and Pepper (1982, p. 52) observed: "In homes where there is mutual respect and consideration, children are bound to feel secure in their parents' love and rarely resort to threats and emotional blackmail."

Developing family themes: Family roles   Individuals internalize an entire set of roles, which their families and their surrounding culture impose upon them. The aim of these roles is to help in categorizing the different family members, while monitoring their family functioning. Roles and the norms associated with them provide much needed order and predictability in the life of any group. Stereotypical family roles, those of mother, father, child and so on, are shaped by the culture in which they are embedded (see, for example, Giovannini, 1998). These roles determine the behaviors and attitudes of the individuals occupying them, thus guaranteeing some degree of cohesion and consistency within and across families. In addition to such basic and necessary roles, each family creates a system of further roles, which simplify relations and categorize each member of the family unit on the basis of a conspicuous trait or behavior. The more flexible these roles, and the more they take into account individual's unique needs and abilities, the healthier they are, enabling their holders to develop within some limits of confidence. When the roles are rigid and unadapted to individuals – the latter are victimized and the system, as a whole, moves toward dysfunctionality.

An often encountered example of role distortions occurring at the basic, universal level is the result of sociocultural forces. In our clinical practice we have met several women (both Jewish and Moslem, often ultra-religious) who, upon becoming mothers, were expected to relinquish their hopes and/or careers and to devote themselves exclusively to their family. While this suited some of them, many others had to choose between deception and frustration. Their counterparts are those liberated women who have a career and contribute to family finances, even though they are still locked in traditional roles of keeping house and raising children, without their partner's cooperation.

Let us turn now to more specific roles, which are likely to differ from family to family. Consider, for instance, *parentified children*, who "are parents to their parents, and fulfil this role at the expense of their own developmentally appropriate needs and pursuits" (Chase, 1999a, p. x; see also Minuchin, 1974, pp. 97–98). Whether parents assign this role out of immaturity or as a result of preoccupation with their marital (or other) conflict, parentified children are likely to suffer long-term effects, ranging from problems in identity development, through anxiety and low self-esteem, to masochistic and narcissistic personality styles (Chase, 1999b, pp. 19–22). An important contribution to both the understanding of parentification and to its therapy was made by Coale (1999, pp. 133–134). She observed that it is not necessarily the performance of some parental functions that hinder children's psychological development, but rather the fact that while these functions are beyond the call of duty, they go unrecognized, unappreciated, and are incongruent with other expectations for their behavior.

A related violation of the boundaries between generations occurs in the *child as spouse* role. A seemingly innocuous example is the father who boasts (to friends as well as to his wife) of people mistaking his 20-year-old daughter for his girlfriend. Yet when a parent, dissatisfied with his/her spousehood, posits a child in the role of a spouse-substitute (sexually or emotionally; see Maddock and Larson, 1995) – the resulting incest destroys healthy family structure, preventing the child from developing according to its needs. This child is exploited as a compensation for the lack of intimacy between the spouses, and will be prevented from actualizing its own capacity for mature love, intimacy, and family life. Sexual incest, as a pathological (and criminal) solution for sexual frustration, is thought to be more prevalent between fathers and daughters. However, children of both sexes are unprotected against the crippling effects of emotional incest.

A different picture emerges in the *child for ever*: parents who fail in coping with their individual or spousal void are unable to ever release their children. They keep themselves involved in every movement and decision of their adolescent child, thus preventing the child's moving toward independence and healthy adult relationships. Every child has two conflicting needs, the healthy need to distance itself from the family of origin and the infantile need to stay protected in the warm nest. The parents of the *child for ever* strongly reinforce their child's emotional (and other) dependence, and punish its sallies toward individuation.

Locked into a pathogenic relationship, children in the above roles are prevented from developing appropriate ties with their peers (and eventually with their adult partners), for all other ties pale when compared to it. This damage to their skill for intimacy can last for a lifetime, further damaging self-esteem and self-actualization. We have met parents who went with their child to enroll in university or took classes with them, others who wrote their adult children's thesis, married couples who took a parent on every family vacation, and of course those who are party to every intimate detail of their child's marriage. Incapacitating myths ("no one will love/understand you as I do"; "I'm your best friend") make therapy difficult because the characters involved enjoy their togetherness too much. Both the myth and the PFP are likely to be transgenerational: the enmeshing mother had been enmeshed herself, and regards this pattern as proof of good parenthood.

It is not unusual for children to be cast into a specific IP role, such as the family's black sheep, clown, weakling, trickster, genius, dumbbell, do-gooder and so on. All of these have stigmas and pain associated with them – not only those denoting failure, but also the ones that are seemingly flattering. While the former are constantly mocked, the latter are under unceasing pressure to live up to their reputation; they are also likely to be envied by their siblings and even by a parent (see Kramer-Moore and Moore, 2002, p. 179).

Adults can also find themselves in distorted roles. In some families the distribution of parental power is considerably skewed. One parent's inputs (more commonly those of the father) are diminished to such an extent that s/he becomes a non-entity for the children, an *insignificant parent*. S/he is left with the formal tasks (such as keeping house or providing), but the children do not regard him or her as a source of influence. Both parents are responsible for this PFP, for the *over-significant parent* seizes the full territory of parenting, while the other one passively relinquishes it. It is often the case that fathers have no opportunity to be emotionally involved in bringing up their children, yet this does not prevent their children from developing expectations, and suffering disappointments with respect to their fathers. The insignificant father – the butt of family jokes, as well as a source of his spouse's power – provides a pathogenic model for his sons as fathers, and for his daughters, as future spouses.

Spousal role distortions occur when the spousal dyad fails to act as an intimate team, breeding a large variety of pathological roles. The factors common to all of these are inequality and the stereotypical, grotesque ex-aggeration of a single personality trait. In complementary relationships the roles are necessarily interdependent: healthy – sick, controller – controlled, pursuer – distancer, strong – weak, active – passive, emotional – rational, success – failure, and so on. In symmetrical spousal dyads both partners opt for the same role: they are both fighters, losers, talkers or basket cases. The competition for role recognition pushes both participants in these PFPs towards escalation. These distortions are likely to have far reaching consequences regarding their children's role perceptions.

Developing family themes: Communication   Satir (1988, p. 51) regarded communication as the largest single factor determining what happens to a person in this world, and what kinds of relationships s/he makes with others (see also Galvin, Bylund, and Brommel, 2008). Every behavior, non-verbal and verbal, carries overt and covert messages, and intrafamilial communication determines the family's quality of life. When open communication is lacking, anger and frustration accumulate, and are expressed in either active or passive aggression. A family in which dinner table conversation is limited to "pass the salt" may tell the therapist that everything is fine, even though their silent IP indicates something else. Another symptom of poor communication within the family system is the frequent use of controlling myths. The two spouses' communication patterns, acquired in their families of origin, set the tone for the next generation, as well. The therapist's role is to facilitate the learning of functional interpersonal communication skills (see Part II).

Developing family themes: Coalitions   "We always start by getting information that you could put under the heading of 'Who is with whom?'" – wrote Milan Systemic family therapist Boscolo (Boscolo et al., 1987, p. 114). Families with healthy coalitions (strong spousal/parental team, well separated from but readily accessible to the strong coalition of siblings) are rarely seen in therapy. Instead, we constantly come across one parent teaming up with one or more of the children, with the other parent either alone or in a firm coalition with another child. Many other alliances form the basis of PFPs, involving the participants' family of origin, their in-laws, as well as extra-familial figures: grandmothers and sisters-in-law, cousins and mates regularly substitute for the much needed intimacy and camaraderie that could be obtained within the age-appropriate strata of the nuclear family. Note that often changing ties and sporadic, short-term connections (quality-time with one of the children, a weekend with the grandparents, or the weekly time-out with a group of friends) are signs of healthy flexibility, as long as they do not interfere with the spouses' ability to enjoy their primary coalition. For the sake of the smooth functioning of the family it is crucial to realize that individuals differ in their needs for separateness vs. togetherness, and that both within and across coalitions these preferences are at times incompatible. If one person's needs become egocentric and supersede those of others, anger, pain and frustration result. If, instead, there is discussion and sensitivity to each other, flexibly functioning coalitions can survive and serve their members' emotional needs.

A further coalition-related issue concerns the spouses' family of origin. Spousal conflicts often revolve around "your family vs. mine": Whose parents are more educated, wealthy or good-looking, whose mother helps more with the children, whose brother is friendlier or better at fixing a roof? Apart from the unhealthy competition that is engendered by them, these comparisons also carry a Layer B message: You and your dowry are worth less than mine. One of the sources of our self-esteem is our roots; degrading one's spouse's family is, in our clinical experience, a perfect method for killing intimacy and love. The PFPs present in these squabbles – belittling, bookkeeping, rivalry – all signal that acceptance of one spouse by the other is conditional. The family therapist's task is to widen the circle of acceptance, to help the spouses relate to each other without putting value tags on traits, behaviors and family connections.

Developing family themes: Insight, reflection, and change   The list of family themes we have treated here is more representative than exhaustive; many others will appear in the course of therapy. As noted above, the goal of family therapy is to reduce pain and to bring about better coping within families. To achieve this, the entire chain of therapeutic activities has to be traversed with every theme that a family presents: Stop, reflect, gain insight into one's current behavior, change, evaluate the results, maintain the new behavior if it suits one's healthy needs. By the time they leave therapy, family members need to be able to answer all of these questions: How do we help each other to change? How do we cope with regression? How do we use the "red flag"? How do we examine whether the change suits us as individuals and as a family? Do we know how to live and let live within the family unit? All of these issues have to be touched upon *in* therapy, so that the family can continue and raise them on their own, *following* therapy.

Stage 3: Evaluation and conclusion

The evaluation of a therapeutic process requires a formative, responsive approach, rather than a summative one. At several points during the course of therapy, family members are encouraged to evaluate their progress as compared with their expectations, and to discuss the different needs associated with "I", "Thou", and "We". Possible clashes among these needs are dealt with through the help of newly acquired communication skills. Thus, evaluation becomes an integral part of therapy itself. The family and the therapist monitor the changes in family structure and dynamics both within the therapeutic milieu and outside it. The final stage of formal therapy occurs with the implementation of newly learned skills in everyday life.

The success of therapy is rarely all or nothing. In some situations a little stopping and reflecting is sufficient, and the clients can continue on their own. In others, there is a lengthy process, with many ups and downs. After a big step forward, there might be a serious regression, demanding more work and sometimes a return to previous themes.

Therapy does not end abruptly. As the family progresses in acquiring more functional communication skills and healthier coping mechanisms, it often becomes possible to space out therapy sessions and to bring about gradual separation. Neither does therapy necessarily end with the cessation of the formal therapeutic relationship. The goal is to maintain the new, functional behavior patterns, gained during therapy, as family members' lifecycles proceed and conditions vary. On the one hand, the positive benefits of the changes encourage the family to maintain them; on the other hand, as stressful situations arise and the family's anxiety level rises – there is a tendency to regress to old, dysfunctional habits. Until the changes are internalized and become an integral part of the family's repertoire, there might be a need for occasional boosting from a therapist. Announcing an open-door policy reassures the family that if need arises, the therapist will be available for them.

Novice therapists are often worried about clients developing dependence on them. In our experience this does not happen; in fact it is mostly clients who initiate the termination of therapy, especially when it is understood that the door is always open for future meetings. It is not unusual to meet a family who had been in therapy and hear them say: "We had a fight and then talked about it", or "We solved a conflict by asking ourselves: how would you have responded?"

There are several, more problematic scenarios. Since therapy cannot be an endless process, we sporadically ask our clients to reflect whether their time (and money) is well spent. A family's feeling of no progress can be due to the therapist's method and personality or to resistance (see Chapter 4). Such immobility needs to be discussed as soon as possible, and if it is not resolved, it is the therapist's responsibility to refer the family. Occasionally a family will find that even though they have further issues, they have solved the immediate, most pressing ones. For some others therapy has become too painful and they need some time to consider whether they want to continue it.

In another difficult scenario, one part of the family makes good progress, while others are stuck. Change cannot be forced, but it is possible to examine what change the resistant client wants. S/he is likely to say: "I'm fine as I am" and "there was no need to do all of this in the first place." Now the rest of the family have to decide whether they want to continue. With one spouse progressing and the other being stuck, separation or divorce may ensue. In such cases the resistant member is angry at the therapist: instead of helping in the cover-up, the therapist has exposed the pain. The therapist's task here is to help all concerned clarify the costs and benefits of their various alternatives, and prevent to his/her best ability self-sacrifice on the part of any family member.

Even in the most problematic scenarios, when many of the family's goals have not been achieved, the mere fact that family members have communicated and are more aware of their controversial stances and needs is a sign that they have made the first step towards identifying entrenched family pain; this may lead to further therapy at a time more appropriate for them.

Activities

1 Family pain mapping

Trigger: Prepare paper and crayons. Draw a map where each "country" is an issue that causes pain in the family. Name them and use size, color, distance from other issues, and so on to characterize each "country." Now place all the maps in the centre of the circle and decide, as a group, which should be talked about first, what comes next (not necessarily in this session). Have each person say something about the chosen pain.

How will the map look if therapy is successful?
Will any country/pain disappear, or just change size, position, etc?

2 Genogram

Trigger: Each family member draws a genogram (see Box 3.2).
Look together at the products, point out different views, gaps, mention the legitimate subjectivity of holding different views of one's family. Then

ask members to use a red pen to add flags where there is pain in the family – either in individual family members or in the connections between them. Point out again the differences, the pains sensed by some and not by others.

How do I contribute to this pain?
What changes should I make to lessen the pain?

3 Roles

Trigger: Each person draws stick figures, representing every family member (including oneself), and adds to each as many hats as needed, indicating all the roles this person has in the family. If needed, give examples (based on your familiarity with the family) beyond father, mother, daughter, and so on, such as finance minister, decorator, builder, peace maker, clown.

Now color red those that cause stress or pain, blue the ones you're comfortable with. Talk about the different perceptions.

Possible points for discussion:

Did I see the roles others have?
Did they see mine?
Which of these roles did I choose freely?
What are the gains and losses of the various roles?

4 A sack of stones

This is a guided imagination activity for couples.

Trigger: Speak slowly in a relaxed, low voice: Sit in a comfortable position, close your eyes, breathe deeply. Imagine a sack of stones of different sizes. These are the things you've brought from your family of origin that are now a source of stress, pain, discomfort. Now draw them in your mind – what size? What color? Are the edges smooth or jagged? When you're ready, open your eyes slowly.

Talk about some of the stones.
What do they mean in your life as an individual and as a part of this family?
What can replace these stones in order to lessen the present family pain?

5 Conflict or What is this quarrel about?

Trigger: Ask family members to write a short script of a typical quarrel in the family: How does it start, who says what to whom, how does it end? [pause]

This is the overt content of the quarrel. But what is it really about? When the content is put aside, what are the underlying agendas? What are the anxieties, hidden motives, past and present? [help family members to identify Layers B and C] Ask yourself: What do I gain and what do I lose in such a quarrel, as an individual and as a member of this family?

6 Windows

This is a guided imagination activity.

Trigger: Darken the room, speak slowly, in a relaxed, low voice: Sit in a comfortable position, close your eyes, breathe deeply. You're standing at a window through which you see a family [of the same composition as this one]. They're happy, close to each other. This is the family you'd like to be a part of. Look at them: What makes them happy? [pause] You didn't know that they were in some serious trouble a year ago, but they've overcome it. What made this possible? [pause] What do you need in your family to be like the one you've just observed? [pause] Breathe deeply, move your limbs, open your eyes slowly. Turn on the lights.

Share with the others your insights, so that they can better understand you. Is there anything you would like to request from them in order to feel better?

4

Making Therapy Work, or Practice What You Preach

Experience is, for me, the highest authority. (Rogers, 1967, p. 23)

Even for us, experienced therapists that we are, every new family can cause accelerated heartbeats. There are always surprises, and often there is no way to foresee the dynamics of a given session. Initial anxiety is important: it keeps us on our toes and prevents arrogance. We bring with us a

Destructive Myths in Family Therapy: How to Overcome Barriers to Communication by Seeing and Saying – A Humanistic Perspective, First Edition. Daniela Kramer-Moore and Michael Moore.
© 2012 John Wiley & Sons, Ltd. Published 2012 by John Wiley & Sons, Ltd.

well-prepared work plan, excitement and motivation, profound faith in the power of empathy and congruent communication, as well as our best therapeutic skills. None of this makes us perfect, and we make mistakes time and again. Reviewing such mistakes and sharing them with our clients has several advantages: it demonstrates that we always need to learn more about the dynamics of ourselves and others, makes us more approachable, and reminds clients that errors can be both made and corrected.

An experienced therapist has little need for most of what follow, while beginners are in need of all the help they can get. The latter especially need supervision, that is, scheduled opportunities to discuss with an experienced therapist what happens in sessions. The following is a mixed bag of helpful ideas; in no way can it replace professional supervision.

The Therapist as Client

We are taught from an early age to put on a mask, a perfect armor, so that no one will see our imperfections. To become a good therapist, who is able to create trust and to contain the "defects" of our clients sympathetically and without judgment, we must be able to identify and to accept our own weaknesses, use them as a means for progress, rather than regress. This stance is crucial; no technique can substitute for it (hence the many not-so-successful therapists). This is why we encourage our students to undergo therapy in general and group therapy in particular. Peer influence to which one is exposed in groups is tremendous, for seeing, listening, and saying (all crucial skills a therapist must have before imparting them to clients) are essential interpersonal processes.

Some therapists project an attitude of omnipotence; armed with their professional knowledge and experience, they suggest that they better understand what suits their clients. Yet neither education, nor years of practice makes a therapist trustworthy for clients. To be able to understand how vulnerable their clients are, therapists must have experienced the anxiety of meeting a stranger, to whom one is expected to expose one's this far well-hidden pains and wounds. To empathize with clients' inevitable regressions, therapists must have been baffled themselves by the paradox of wanting to change yet apparently acting against one's own interest. We recall a client for whom it took eight months to bring up his sister's suicide, and his finding her body, when he was a child. Expecting such unexpected revelations without judgment (thus accepting the client's right to wait for a long time before confiding in us) becomes easier when therapists have occupied the client's seat themselves and have experienced the difficulty of revealing sensitive information.

Another important result of having undergone therapy is the improved ability to recognize and deal with unfinished business and countertransference, that is, therapists' tendency to project their own agendas into those of the clients. It is vital for the therapist to stop and reflect on the difficulty of separating his or her own narrative from the clients'. Honest, continuous self-examination is one of the keys to the development of a significant therapeutic relationship. The better a therapist knows and accepts self, the less judgmental and more authentic s/he will be. There are no shortcuts: warmth, empathic understanding, a non-judgmental stance and a well-differentiated self must come from inside. Those who are in this position realize that they are not omnipotent and can proceed with modesty.

Neutrality, Empathy, Authenticity, and Creativity

Here are some key attributes therapist will find necessary for their work:

- *Neutrality* Many clients expect the family therapist to be an arbitrator who will decide who is in the right, and who deserve to be told to change their ways. It is the therapist's duty to make it clear at the very beginning that there are no guilty vs. innocent parties, that family members are doing their best to survive and satisfy their individual needs. This step often turns the tables: those who have been seemingly compliant, hoping for the therapist to change others, are now disappointed, and become less compliant. The ones who were dragged into therapy start to see that someone may listen to them without judging them and their motivation to cooperate increases. The therapist needs to be consistently non-judgmental, without taking sides or being sucked into the conflicts presented. Neutrality (referred to by Bowen, 1978, p. 79 as "a position of unbiased detachment") is an absolute necessity in order for all members of a conflict ridden family to trust the therapist.

  Yet we all tend to take sides and each client is likely to try and enlist the therapist's support; all of this makes neutrality difficult to maintain. Clients, basically interested in their own gains, must be shown that in the long run the present situation is one of lose–lose, and that they can all gain by allowing for change to occur (see Chapter 5 for the dangers of *homeostasis*). The controlling father of a depressed adolescent or the perfectionist mother of the anorectic teenager will not let go of their hold, unless they fully understand that soon they may not have a child to control at all. This knowledge usually comes too late. If the therapist informs them of the danger, s/he will be seen as an enemy. However, if s/he connects with controlling parents through empathy, helping them express their anxiety over the redundancy they imagine they will experience if their child becomes more independent, showing them the transgenerational roots of their situation, then these parents can start separating their needs from those of the child. This differentiation is essential for a positive outcome. Individuation is a basic condition of mental health and one of the goals of family therapy; one way of demonstrating it is through the therapist's neutral and well-differentiated stance. One of the first steps of therapy is the untangling of family mass, and the understanding of every member's needs. Whenever the therapist is sucked into a coalition, s/he renders the other family members more resistant. A consistently impartial stance by a therapist is not only a necessity for the achievement of therapeutic goals, it also serves as a model for dealing with engulfing relationships within the family.

- *Empathy* A main goal of therapy is functional, healthy communication; a crucial ingredient of the latter is empathy (see Box 3.1, pp. 34–35). Empathy makes it possible for individuals to see not only themselves but others as well, from their inner vantage point, to listen to them without judging, with warmth and understanding, and to verbalize this empathic attitude. Box 4.1 is an example of the need for empathic listening.

Box 4.1 Listen!

The following has been attributed to various sources, among them Carl Rogers.

Listen!
When I ask you to listen to me and you start giving advice you have not done what I have asked.
When I ask you to listen to me and you begin to tell me why I shouldn't feel that way you are trampling on my feelings.

(continued)

When I ask you to listen to me and you feel you have to do something
to solve my problem you have failed me. Strange as that may seem.

Listen!
All I asked was that you listen, not talk or do, but hear me.
I can do for myself, I am not helpless: maybe discouraged and faltering,
maybe lonely and isolated and grieving and searching, but not helpless.
When you do something for me that I can and need to do myself you
contribute to my fear and my weakness.
But when you accept as a simple fact that I do feel what I feel, no matter
how irrational it seems to you, then I can quit trying to convince you and
get about the business of understanding what's behind this irrational
feeling, and when that is clear the answers are obvious and I don't need
advice.

So please listen and just hear me and if you want to talk wait a minute
for your turn and I will listen to you.

An empathic therapist is, at one and the same time, both a supportive
character, worthy of trust and honest sharing, and an important role model.
Whenever s/he expresses feelings, provides feedback, suggests alternative
modes of communication, it should be done from an empathic stance. In
our experience, psychotherapy trainees are as amazed as clients when they
first encounter empathic attitudes. They soon find that this is what they need
and what they missed heretofore, and what they do not find in most other
social circles. Those who train themselves for therapy should go through
extended training in empathic communication, as well. We are bound to
ask whether clients can rely on non-empathic therapists. In our opinion
they are ineffective and should not offer therapy.

To be honest, all of us have a limit to our empathic capability. As a rule,
we cannot be empathic when we are anxious. Some therapists will not be
able to work with pedophiles, others with murderers, or with the parents
of an anorectic teenager. The first two of these would be difficult for most
of us; the third one could be the result of a personal tragedy. Every client
deserves to be treated with empathy, thus therapists should choose between
going into therapy themselves, so as to cope with these anxieties and to
widen their limits of empathy before treating others with similar issues, or
expressing this limitation and referring their clients. Becoming empathic is

a lifelong process for all of us, with ups and downs, according to both our clients and our personal circumstances; it is a topic which must be attended to throughout our professional life.

- *Authenticity* This is another necessary quality (see Chapter 6). Therapy is inherently intimate; the basis for intimate relationships is honest sharing of thoughts and feelings. However, being genuine, honest, real and transparent (all of these have something in common with authenticity) does not mean that one has to say everything. We find ourselves at the middle of a continuum that ranges from the Rogerian position of saying very little (see Rogers, 1990e) to a point where the therapist divulges every thought and feeling s/he has about the clients. Therapists might see and hear things to which they would rather not respond either at that time or at all, unless directly asked. Thus s/he may find a comment appropriate for one member of the family but premature for another, or may ask not to be drawn out on his or her private issues either because s/he deems them to be irrelevant or in order not to steal the stage. Apart from this everything is open for discussion (unless one of the clients objects; see *Agreement*, below), including the therapist's decision not to open a specific topic at a specific time.

  In their role as models for interpersonal communication family therapists set an example here for their clients, for the same limits are applicable to inter- and intragenerational communication within the family. Parents do not discuss some private matters with their children; children should not be expected to share every corner of their private life with the adults; spouses should similarly respect each other's right to a private world, while realizing that keeping secrets within the spousal relationships is costly to intimacy.

- *Creativity* This is the quality needed to realize Yalom's earlier mentioned idea of inventing a new therapy for every client. After years of working as therapists, many agendas reoccur; some narratives we hear appear to be repetitions of the ones we heard in the past. This is a trap, for while the basic problems may be similar, their solutions are an intricate function of the history, personality, and interpersonal dynamics of the individuals involved. Then there are also surprises during the process. The presenting problem disappears and something else takes its place, there are unforeseen progresses, followed by regressions. Therefore therapist's flexibility and creativity are essential for the creation of a different therapy for every family, at every stage, suited to the current issue. The creative attitude has no assumptions; every family is learned afresh, with some trial and error about what works, what creates progress. We are pluralistic in our theoretical framework; ready to experiment, offering structured as well as unstructured therapy, both verbal and non-verbal triggers. This stops us from becoming mere technicians and renders every therapy and every client unique.

The Therapeutic Agreement

The overt purpose of the Agreement (see Box 4.2 and Activity 1, below) is to provide a safety net for clients by creating conditions that permit a productive dialogue. But there is also a covert, Layer B, purpose: negotiating the agreement and exposing one's anxieties about therapy offer the family an opportunity for teamwork around sensitive topics. The Agreement is produced early in the sequence of therapy sessions; family members need to realize that family therapy is not just about I or you, but rather about cooperation for the achievement of a common goal.

Box 4.2 An outline for a family therapy agreement

A. Setting
  1. Place, days, hours.
  2. Number of sessions prior to first evaluation (ca. 6–8).
  3. Rules of attendance, absence, inviting extended family members (only if all agree and are prepared), stopping therapy.
  4. Sessions with individual, couple, siblings, or entire family.
  5. Family members will negotiate ways to end therapy and possible follow-up.
  6. Other.
B. Rights and obligations within the therapy session
  1. The right to privacy, the right to keep silent.
  2. The right to personal pace.
  3. The right "to flag" both entire topics and single utterances.
  4. The right to set limits.
  5. The obligation to show up or to cancel in advance.

(continued)

6. The obligation to actively participate or voice one's choice not to participate.
7. The obligation to listen to others with respect.
8. The obligation to provide honest feedback.
9. The obligation to ask within a session for changes in this agreement if unsatisfactory to any family member.
10. The obligation to respect this agreement.
11. Other.

C. Rights and obligations between therapy sessions
1. Discussions started in sessions may be continued at home, with mutual consent (but see the following item).
2. Family members should not use against each other confidential material that came up in session. If this happens the hurt person can "flag" the other(s).
3. Family members may reveal, to outsiders, intimate details learned during session only about themselves while protecting the confidence of other family members.
4. Other.

D. Relations between family members and therapist
1. The therapist will do his or her best to give authentic feedback to the family members.
2. The therapist is obliged to keep content of session (except for criminal behavior or intent, as required by law) confidential both during therapy and after its termination. Therapists may consult their supervisor about dilemmas providing the family's anonymity is respected.
3. The relationship between family members and the therapist will be purely professional, without any socializing.
4. To prevent family members talking behind each other's back, telephone contacts can take place only in an emergency or for rescheduling a session.
5. Any comforting touch by therapist needs prior consent.
6. The therapist will not divulge information gained in one configuration of the family to another (e.g. from children to parents or from one spouse to another).

(continued)

> 7. The therapist will refer the family if there is either no progress being made or s/he feels unequipped to deal with their problem.
> 8. The therapist will be available to the family for future consultation.
> 9. Other.

At this stage clients are encouraged to reflect with regard to the ensuing therapy:

What do I need, what do I want, what am I afraid of?
What are my limits, when do I close up and stop cooperating?

Anxieties about therapy are bound to be voiced. The most common ones are:

others might gain from therapy but I'll certainly lose;
pain will increase, the family will disintegrate;
therapist may take sides;
therapist may talk about us to outsiders;
others might use against me what I reveal here;
I'll be forced to reveal things I don't want to talk about;
if others won't open up as much as I, I'll feel foolish;
I won't be understood and I'll be misjudged.

The therapist's task is to facilitate this negotiation, to suggest overlooked but necessary points, to suggest options (e.g. "raise a flag" when a rule is broken). It is crucial for every family member to be satisfied that a safe environment has been created for him/her:

they will be listened to without censorship;
the therapist will not judge emotions as right or wrong;
anxiety is natural;
events need not be experienced identically by different persons;
each person's pace is different; and
everyone is entitled not to reveal what they wish to keep private.

The agreement is verbal (except for suicidal youth, where a written agreement may be prepared with the adolescent without the parents), and may be renegotiated when need arises.

Types of Clients

The uniqueness of every family need not stop us from considering some frequently encountered types of clients and examining their probable motivation.

- The *resistance* of some clients to cooperate with the therapist is not as paradoxical as it sounds: Ackerman et al. (1991), for instance, discussed the problems arising when a family is referred for treatment because of child abuse. Other involuntary clients include the husband who was dragged into therapy by his wife, and the teenage daughter, whose rebelliousness does not permit her to listen to adults. Clients from choice and clients from necessity have different starting points: the former realize that something is causing them misery and ask to undergo a process, even if it is painful, in order to discover the source of their misery. Having consciously taken the risk of "seeing" these clients are one step ahead. The latter resist seeing because they feel threatened about losing control over their family, learning unpleasant things about themselves or seeing their relationships unravel (see Golden, 1985, for a cognitive-behavioral account of the main sources of client resistance). Resistance can take many forms. "I don't believe in psychology" is a not uncommon loophole through which unwilling clients try to escape. Other types of resistance are the repetition of what others say, smiles, saying either nothing significant or being sarcastic, as well as continuous silence.

  There is no magic bullet that solves the problem of resistance. For the family therapist to be able to address it, s/he must first understand and empathize with the anxieties that lie behind a person's resistance. The Agreement, discussed above, is often a useful tool that alleviates specific anxieties; so does the safe, empathic environment offered in therapy sessions. It is important for initially resistant clients (as for compliant ones) to experience being seen and heard non-judgmentally, perhaps for the first time in their life. Once they feel that the therapist is there for all of them, and that some small changes are taking place in family communication, they are likely to become more relaxed and receptive.

- *Placators* flatter the therapist, agree with everything. They are easy to like, the atmosphere is pleasant, but very little gets done. Often this is but another type of resistance, a defense where the client makes sure nothing painful will happen. We reflect this to clients ("a good time was had by all" does not advance them) and examine with them the gains and losses of employing this style both inside and outside therapy.
- Some *passive* clients who had no experience of therapy and know nothing about it are willing to talk mostly about their daily routine. They (as well as novice therapists) will greatly benefit from the *Activities* which minimize the possibility of escaping to irrelevant topics. Once they learn the language, these clients may not need further "triggers."
- Pincus and Dare (1978, p. 36) drew attention to the purportedly "healthy" partner, who brings the "ill" one to therapy: "Change him/her, make him/her well!" Unaware of their own part in the situation, such clients hold on to a fantasy in which therapy will improve their life without any cost to themselves. Pincus and Dare attributed this ploy to projections of repressed needs and drives onto the partner and regarded it as a destructive process which may underlie a great many marital and family problems: "In spite of appearances to the contrary, the 'illness' is in fact shared between the two, the 'well' partner maintaining his well-being through the co-operation of the other partner who ostensibly carries the illness."

Stopping and Reflecting

The need to stop and reflect has been briefly mentioned in Chapter 1. Taking seemingly trivial things, heretofore unquestioned, and examining what lies behind them, asking whether "they work," might be natural for the therapist, but is a new skill for most clients. Let us stop and look at routine fights between spouses or between parents and children: What does each participant want and need, what would they say if they were entirely frank? This is a chance to create a more congruent narrative. Next, let us reflect. This goes deeper than the previous examination. Where have I seen this pattern of behavior before? How did this serve or disserve the participants? Does this serve me? What does it do to my relationship, what does the other person involved feel/think? Then comes choice. Do I want to change? Will I gain or lose by changing? If willing to change, what are my options? What are the costs and benefits of each alternative course of action?

Stopping and reflecting should be intrinsic to therapists' private and professional life; if they do not do this, they cannot help clients master it.

Implementing Change

Therapy triggers a process aimed at insight and the development of interpersonal skills. The therapist's task is not to steer clients toward some well-defined, externally imposed goal, but rather to create a climate where individuals can choose their own goals, as well as the pace and route to achieve them (see the basics of the humanistic approach in Rogers, 1990a). It is thus crucial for therapists to let go of the reins, to provide stimuli for work, and to back off; having set the process in motion, they are mostly observers, intervening only in order to clarify, to focus, and to keep the clients on track. Therefore therapists should come with a willingness to activate the family or couple who have asked for help, should not *work instead of* them, *for them* or *against them*, but *be there for* them. At the conclusion of therapy clients often announce that the therapist has transformed their life. We always rephrase this: Though we held the torch, it was the clients who took the difficult route. Successful therapy is the clients' achievement.

The various approaches to family therapy differ in the degree of direct involvement. The more active ones (such as cognitive-emotional, behavioral, paradoxical, or positive psychology) are too controlling in our opinion; they thrust too much of their ideology on the clients, without sufficiently respecting their world. We have found that in addition to Rogerian empathic listening, we can also voice our impression of what is going on, carefully giving the clients a chance to reject it, if it does not suit them. We prefer never to miss an opportunity to point out communication blockers in the here-and-now. Therapy, in addition to examining the roots of a dysfunctional pattern, also serves as a dynamic learning laboratory where clients and therapist stop and reflect on every problematic utterance, examining its costs and benefits.

Achieving change in the safe environment of the therapy room is but a first step of a long process. Clients who have apparently acquired the skill of empathic listening in the therapy room, will start giving advice at home; those who have learned what authenticity means will mask their feelings toward their family. The process of transferring change from the therapy session to the outside world is fraught with regressions, frustrations, drawbacks, and anxieties. This process is made even more complicated by the different pace of each family member. Some seem to have been waiting for the occasion and burst forward. Others show resistance, express disappointment, and take much longer to gain insight. Going too fast frightens clients; going too slowly creates disappointment. The therapist's strongest tool, in this dilemma, as everywhere else, is empathy: going with each client at his/her own pace, with a flashlight in hand, throwing light on dark spots. S/he is a guest in a home who enters only the rooms into which s/he is invited.

Sad and disappointing as it may be, some families leave therapy without having benefitted from it. This may be due to deep-rooted homeostatic resistance on the part of a powerful family member, to a personality disorder that is not amenable to family therapy, or to some basic mismatch between the family and the therapist. It is unrealistic to hope to be able to create a lasting change in the life of every potential client.

Individual vs. Family Therapy

To be a focused, empathic supporter, therapists must see their client's narrative from the client's point of view. In family therapy the therapist meets not one but several interlaced narratives. So even though individual therapy and therapy with several clients are similar in many ways (for example, both require empathy, authenticity, and the stop-reflect sequence), the dynamics are different. On the one hand, the issue of building trust is more difficult when several clients are present. Anxieties may be higher, and so are the needs to use old defense mechanisms; there is a further difficulty to be authentic because of the danger of exposing one's pains to those who may be causing them. One is afraid that issues brought to light in session will be used against oneself outside the session. Add to this the often encountered see-saw phenomenon: As one member of the group becomes stronger, another weakens. On the other hand, when the entire family unit is in therapy, a degree of intimacy is created, a public commitment is made. Since every single narrative might (and often does) clash with that of others, and since these narratives are always interwoven, the possibility to empathically listen to each other produces family cohesion and removes some of the dependence on the therapist as "the only person who understands me." When the family learns basic rules of teamwork, they can use this skill outside therapy to help and support each other. Furthermore, the fact that family issues are dealt with openly rather than behind each other's back, teaches openness and functional communication skills. They can assist each other to stop and reflect, thus speeding up the therapeutic process. In this situation the IP is likely to be relieved of his/her role, and the entire system takes responsibility for what is happening. Naturally, this cannot happen in individual therapy. These basic differences between individual vs. family orientation are at the very centre of Bowen's approach to family psychotherapy: "psychotherapy directed at the hypothesized emotional oneness within the family" (1978, p. 75; see also a similar opinion in Minuchin, 1974, p. 111).

The question of who participates in family therapy has a complicated answer. Some family therapists insist on everyone being present, others are ready to work with whoever is available. Our policy is influenced by two basic principles:

- The adults, both as parents and as spouses, bear most of the responsibility for dysfunctionality within the family, so they are the principal clients.
- It is important to maintain clear boundaries between generational sub-systems (see Minuchin (1974, pp. 51–60).

As a result, we tend to spend more time with the parents than with the children, and more time with generational subsystems than with the entire family unit. The demands of specific situations make creativity and flexibility into key components here, as well: at times the therapist wishes to work with the entire family, but one or more of the members refuse to come. In other cases, families insist on coming to therapy together, but the therapist needs to work with a particular member on matters of separation/individuation. Secrets such as incest or adultery are unlikely to be revealed in the presence of some members; children, especially adolescents are similarly reluctant to talk about their parents in the latter's presence.

A Few Words on Group Psychotherapy

When a couple is not available for therapy (as in the case of a spouse refusing to participate), or in the case of individuals (often troubled adolescents) seeking help, we find that group therapy (with the group composed of unrelated individuals, sharing some common problem) is preferable to individual therapy. The group provides an opportunity for feedback and reinforcement from a more or less close social circle. Mainly when the issues revolve around communication, the group has far more power than sessions with an individual. Group therapy (see especially Yalom, 1991, 1995) has an infinite range of possibilities. In our experience individuals in groups reach insights in a single session, which they did not gain through years of individual therapy. When in a group, participants are exposed to processes similar to those encountered in the family. There is a chance for experiencing new communication skills and "corrections," with the added benefit of a trained facilitator who can stop futile fights and focus discussion on relevant issues.

The actual work in the group also consists of stopping, reflecting, experimenting with new behavior patterns and arriving at insights through direct feedback. Content is provided by group members; these tend to focus on some universal agendas, with other group members recognizing their own relevant issues. Advantages include the richness of situations, options, experiences. Pluralistic views and empathic attitudes towards others have a chance to develop, more and more varied interactions are made possible. While being more varied than just one family system and a more realistic microcosm than the one a client might find at home, there are also clear disadvantages: Participants (often women) become frustrated. "Why am I not understood, appreciated at home, the way I'm here, among my peers?" Individuals may come to prefer the group at the expense of their family, for the intimacy and cohesion the former provides. So, our first choice would always be family (or couple) therapy where the family who live as a unit go through the therapeutic change as a unit, but group therapy dedicated to family topics (spousal and parental) comes as a close second.

In both family and group therapy the presence of a co-therapist is a great advantage. We have found that a mixed-gender therapist team can demonstrate many important themes concerning communication; at the same time there is less danger of one family member feeling isolated, and the richness and variety of another point of view is always beneficial to clients. When they process a session, co-therapists can also help each other expose blind-spots and countertransferences.

About the Activities

Clients will often say: "We can now see the problem, but we can't change, we're unable to perform like this at home!" Since we are in favor of short treatment, proactiveness is needed; this is offered by the "Activities" at the end of each chapter. These are triggers to think differently, to experience new ways of behaving, to gain both insights and training for alternative behaviors. We find that some families are able to use these activities on their own at home after a few sessions, and some actually ask for "homework" and come back to the next session with the results. Here, too, every therapist will do different things. Various ways to activate clients are abundant (see drama, play, art, music, biblio, narrative therapies). All of these can be incorporated here, depending on the therapist's abilities, inclinations and experience. In all of these the families do not talk about a problem or its solution from an external point of reference but experience it, live it through. Every therapist is invited to add his or her own favorite method to make therapy more effective. We find being creative and inventing new activities as a refreshing and stimulating way to counteract burnout.

It is important to provide pleasant, warm, comfortable surroundings and to give some thought to seating arrangements, to lighting, and to décor. The therapist should make sure sessions can proceed undisturbed by external noise or uninvited visitors. In several cases spatial arrangements become important and there is need to have sufficient room to move about.

Many activities necessitate some simple preparation: paper, pencils, crayons or other accessories may be needed; a short paragraph may have to be printed out. Occasionally, there is a connection between two consecutive activities; clients can be reminded to bring something for the following meeting; some "homework," given at a previous session can be referred to. Though the activities are planned for work with families, most can be adapted to different types of therapy: individual, couple, or group.

It is essential to pick the activities one feels comfortable with, while best serving the family's needs, composition (genders, generations, ages), and abilities (both emotional and intellectual). The activities offered in any chapter greatly differ in terms of depth and therapeutic skills needed. The therapist's skill level and the climate (level of trust, rapport, intimacy) that has been created should help make the right choices. Most of the activities contain a selection of *possible points for discussion*. Discussing too many points in a single session creates superficiality, so the focus needs be only on the most relevant ones.

Multicultural Perspective

We live and operate in multicultural societies. Inevitably, every family therapist will come in contact with clients whose cultural background is different from his or her own. Before expressing our opinion on how to deal with the conflict that ensues, we invite the reader to peruse Box 4.3 for the opinions of several contemporary theorists and practitioners of family therapy.

Box 4.3   How to deal with cultural diversity?

Relativists

- When discussing the influence of cultural differences on the practice of family therapy Lyness, Haddock, and Zimmerman's (2003) reminded therapists of the importance of keeping "this perspective in mind when the client's culture is different from that of the therapist so that the therapist does not misinterpret as pathological behavior which may be culturally based." The example they give is that of Asian-American families indulging their children more than is typical in US culture. Yet both the advice to keep "this perspective in mind" and the mild example fail to address the ethical quandary of the therapist facing harsher clashes of cultures.
- Carr (2006, p. 45) devoted about half-a-page to "class, creed and colour," and there he advocates sensitivity to race and class and an acceptance that "different patterns of organisation, belief systems, and ways of being in the broader sociocultural context may legitimately typify families from different cultures," further adding that, "We must also be sensitive to the fact that we share a responsibility for the oppression of minority groups."
- Sommers-Flanagan and Sommers-Flanagan's (2009) text urges readers to gain "cultural competence," and introduces them to several religious and cultural traditions. For example, *machismo* and *marianismo* are given as central notions of Hispanic/Latino American cultures, though they "are not generally socially acceptable gender-role guidelines in the dominant culture in the United States" (Sommers-Flanagan and Sommers-Flanagan, 2009, p. 413; see also Sue and Sue, 2008).

Universalists

- In a book co-authored by Minuchin, the founder of Structural Family Therapy, there is a chapter titled "All families are different," and another "All families are alike." Both of these notions should make one cautious vis-à-vis "multicultural counseling." Here is their conclusion regarding this issue: "We welcome today's concern for diversity as a significant raiser of consciousness about the

(continued)

dangers of imposing majority values on minority populations. But we also think that there is an element of danger in that politically correct social attitude – a kind of reverse bigotry. As therapists, we are always working with people who are different from us. So we need to account for our own ignorance and our assumptions about people who are different. We need to incorporate the present ethos for understanding diversity, but while accepting that, we also need to recognize that there are universals" (Minuchin, Lee, and Simon, 1996, p. 28).

- A similar opinion was voiced by Nichols and Schwartz (2006). While emphasizing the value of sensitivity to the influence of ethnicity, they found that "segregation, even in the name of ethnic pride, isolates people and breeds prejudice. Perhaps *pluralism* is a better term than *multiculturalism* because it implies more balance between ethnic identity and connection to the larger group" (p. 288; see also Becvar and Becvar, 2009, p. 120).

While our sympathies lie with the universalists, we suggest to go a step further: Sensitivity – yes; value-free therapy – no. Like any other meaningful interaction, therapy is always value-laden. Therapists cannot be completely free of their own worldview, culture, ethnicity and psychological school of thought. For clients, in their turn, the very act of seeking therapy is a value statement. It is, however, the therapist's duty to clarify his/her orientation and to prepare the client for what is coming. Many (perhaps most) clients will not know the sometimes minor, often major differences among the various therapeutic persuasions (see the list at the beginning of Chapter 3). Undoubtedly, all this places the family therapist in an ethical quandary: how does one respect clients whose family-related values diametrically clash with those of the therapist (with respect to, say, equality in general, and women's rights in particular, discussed, along with culturally approved corporal punishment of children in Chapter 7)? Or consider the issue of authenticity and congruence (discussed in Chapter 6): for those who must always be polite, pleasant and placating, authenticity may be considered as "cheek" or impoliteness; an insistence on authentic communication may create problems and even feelings of guilt. In our opinion respecting such clients means referring them to someone else (a classical case of avoidance-avoidance conflict, where leaving the field is the only solution); the last thing a family in pain needs is a cultural conflict with the therapist.

Activities

The following activities serve two purposes: they are directed toward the personal and professional development of the family therapist; with some adjustment, each can be turned into a meaningful activity for clients, as well (especially the first two: Agreement and Listen!).

1 Agreement

An agreement is a must. Before asking family members to suggest their version, try to do it yourself.

Trigger: Place yourself in the client's chair and draft an agreement with an imaginary therapist (using the outline in Box 4.2) that would make you feel safe.

Reflect on the points that you have found significant.
What past experiences made these points stand out?
Your future clients come with different experiences; think of points that may be important for them.
To assist in this task when working with a family, suggest that each of them imagine the worst case scenario and prepare a list of the conditions needed to avoid it.

2 Listen!

Trigger: Read out to yourself "Listen!" (Box 4.1).

Mark the sentence which indicates what you miss or have missed most in your family. Using another color then mark the sentence indicating what is most difficult for you to provide to some of your family members.

Reflect on the different types of listening in your family.
What would you need in order to listen with empathy to the family member you find most difficult to deal with?

3 Good cop, bad cop

Trigger: This is a guided imagination activity. Darken the room, and imagine the following: You've wanted to go into therapy for a long time. Now you're near the door and you hope that it will be opened by the best therapist you can imagine, one to whom you can safely open up and with whom you can share your most embarrassing and painful thoughts and emotions. Reflect: What qualities and behaviors does this therapist have? Breathe deeply a few times while you knock on the door. [pause] The door opens, you're ushered in, and within a few minutes you realize that you've drawn the worst therapist, one with whom you won't be able to share anything meaningful. Reflect: What makes you distrust this therapist? Breathe deeply, move your limbs, open your eyes slowly. Turn on the lights.

What do I need to develop in order to become the "good therapist"?
Under what conditions might I become the "bad therapist", the one who cannot be trusted?

4 The four Fs

Trigger: Place four big signs in the corners of the room, with one of the four Fs: freeze, fly, fight, face up, written on each. Walk from corner to corner, and make a list of the type of people who make you choose each of these reactions.

Possible points for reflection:

Who in my life makes me react with one of the four Fs?
What is it in them that does this?
From whom have I learned this reaction as a child?
What are the gains and losses of this strategy for me and for those around me?
What do I need in order to move to "facing-up"?
What is the implication of the above for my functioning as a family therapist?

5 Empathy training

Trigger: Sit down and place an empty chair in front of yourself. Close your eyes and think of a client who might make (or has made) you angry, disgusted, or fearful.

Open your eyes and tell this imagined person everything you felt towards him or her. Now move to the other chair, close your eyes, and "listen" to what has been said. Stop and reflect: Try and see this person's world from "within," connect to the feelings of failure, isolation, despair.

Now return to the therapist's chair. Put aside his or her traits and acts, and reflect only on what the other person felt when hearing you.

Part II

Saying

The Power of Words

Say what you mean and mean what you say.

We have devoted the first part of this book to the crucially important ability to *see*. When we gain this ability we often verbalize our newly gained

Destructive Myths in Family Therapy: How to Overcome Barriers to Communication by Seeing and Saying – A Humanistic Perspective, First Edition. Daniela Kramer-Moore and Michael Moore.
© 2012 John Wiley & Sons, Ltd. Published 2012 by John Wiley & Sons, Ltd.

knowledge to ourselves, yet in interpersonal affairs this is insufficient. Insight is but the prerequisite for what we must do next: *Say*, or act upon the information we gained through healthy communication with others. It is tempting to take words lightly, to go along with the "Sticks and stones may break my bones, but words will never hurt me" adage; yet by doing so we do injustice to the tremendous power of words. Communication between human beings is achieved first and foremost through the use of words. Think about encouragement, flattery, and forgiving; consider threats, warnings, reproofs and criticisms. And how about tirades and lectures, tributes and compliments, praises and eulogies? A simple "well done!" can put one on the right track, just as a "cut it out!" can put one off for a long time. The crucial role of communication within families is indisputable; Fincham (2004, p. 83), for example, found that "the most common reason for which people seek professional help is relationship problems, and poor communication is the relationship problem most frequently identified by couples." In a similar vein, Laurse and Collins (2004, p. 343) quote empirical research to support their conclusion: "Those who do not learn to communicate effectively when [their] children are young are at risk for dysfunctional discord during adolescence."

Though the variety of communication is endless, it is possible to identify some recurrent patterns. From the several attempts that have been made (see, for example, Trenholm and Jensen, 2004) we find the classification suggested by Satir (1983, 1988) especially useful, both because of its distinct family orientation and its clarity. In our experience, once clients become familiar with Satir's communication patterns, they immediately spot the different types they encounter in their family and have no trouble recognizing transgenerational aspects (*I remember my mother saying that*).

Satir described four dysfunctional communication patterns; we will frequently come across these in the sayings that form the basis of the rest of this book: *Placating* entails striving to please others. To avoid interpersonal conflict, placators blame themselves for whatever goes wrong ("How could I've been so stupid!" or "I should've known better"). *Blaming* is the exact opposite: blamers constantly find fault with others, rejecting their own responsibility ("It's all your fault!", and "Next time be more careful!"). Another pattern used for masking one's vulnerability and inability to cope with conflict is being *Super-reasonable*. In this pattern both one's own emotions and those of others are disregarded. Super-rational communicators are detached; instead of empathizing with their spouse, child or friend, they analyze the problem they are presented with ("There is a perfect logical explanation for that!", or "Statistically, the probabilities are . . ."). Some therapists use interpretations which are super-rational to cover up their lack of empathy, thus demonstrating poor communication skills. The fourth dysfunctional communication pattern is being *Irrelevant*. The technique employed here is distraction: Either by clowning, or by a sudden, whimsical change of topic, irrelevant communicators divert attention from the conflict at hand ("Have I told you the joke about . . . ?" or "Isn't this hot spell something?").

There is a fifth, functional pattern of interpersonal communication, in which there is no need to conceal one's feelings or to escape from an exposure to the emotions of others. In *congruent* communication, also referred to as leveling or flowing, "all parts of the message are going in the same direction: the voice's words match the facial expression, body position, and voice tone. Relationships are easy, free, and honest, and people feel few threats to self-esteem. This response relieves any need to placate, blame, retreat into a computer, or be in perpetual motion" (Satir, 1988, p. 93; more about congruence and authenticity in Chapter 6).

A concept strongly related to congruent communication is the *I-Message*. When confronted with an interpersonal conflict, it is far more effective to express one's emotions and beliefs clearly and honestly, in a non-blameful manner ("I feel uncomfortable when people raise their voice at me"), than to point a finger at the other ("Look what you've done"). "Your I-Message must be *congruent*," wrote Gordon and Edwards, (1995, p. 112), "that is, your *inner experience* and its *outer expression* must match." (It was Thomas Gordon, a clinical psychologist and a student of Carl Rogers, who introduced the I-Message concept in the 1960s.)

The sayings we have chosen to examine in the following chapters are but a small sample of the hurtful, dysfunctional utterances commonly used in many families. (Read more about family myths in Kramer-Moore and Moore, 2002, p. 163–170.) These myths and clichés are often used unthinkingly, without their source taking note of the damage they cause their audience. This damage is twofold: the target is harmed directly, and s/he, as well as other witnesses to the event, learn a communication pattern which they will almost inevitably put into use toward others. Whether children are the direct targets or just all-ears bystanders, when an adult uses such sayings as we will examine, transgenerational transmission is likely to take place.

So let us all think twice before we use any of the sayings that follow.

5

Homeostatic Messages, or Don't Rock the Boat!

When something is festering in your memory or your imagination, laws of silence don't work, it's just like shutting a door and locking it on a house on fire in hope of forgetting that the house is burning. But not facing a fire doesn't put it out. Silence about a thing just magnifies it. It grows and festers in silence, becomes malignant. (Tennessee Williams, 1957, pp. 28–29)

Destructive Myths in Family Therapy: How to Overcome Barriers to Communication by Seeing and Saying – A Humanistic Perspective, First Edition. Daniela Kramer-Moore and Michael Moore.
© 2012 John Wiley & Sons, Ltd. Published 2012 by John Wiley & Sons, Ltd.

Though strictly speaking homeostasis ("same state," in plain English) is the end *product* living organisms are said to strive for, the term is more often used to describe the *process* needed for its achievement. The OED definition of homeostasis is "The maintenance of a dynamically stable state within a system." A good example of physiological homeostasis is the preservation of constant body heat: the healthy human body is able to maintain a temperature of 98.6 degrees, whether it is in the Tropics or at the Arctic Circle.

According to several of the most respected sources of psychological theory, striving for homeostasis is a basic principle of psychology, no less than of physiology. Some have gone as far as to call it "a unifying concept in personality theory" and "the bedrock of personality functioning" (Stagner, 1951, 1977, respectively).

What later came to be known as homeostasis was recognized by the nineteenth century founder of psychophysiology Gustav Fechner as the "principle of constancy" (in Freud, 1955, p. 8), according to which systems have a tendency to either inertia or at least some regularity. Once this quietude is disturbed, systems will attempt to recreate it and to reach stability again.

Freud was greatly impressed by Fechner's notion of constancy and gave it a crucial role in his psychoanalytic theory (e.g. 1955 and 1961). The very basis of psychological development lies in the Id's pursuit of the pleasure principle, that is, its need to reduce tension once it is raised by either internal or external forces: "The mental apparatus endeavours to keep the quantity of excitation present in it as low as possible or at least to keep it constant" (Freud, 1955).

Allport's (1937) theory of personality is to a large extent founded on "the constant return of all psychological systems to a state of equilibrium" (p. 349). In this theory personality is governed by a homeostatic principle of congruence. The latter is provided by what might be called the self. A person's self (sometimes referred to as the proprium) is responsible for the congruence of personality and for the unification of the various behavioral aspects of the individual. *Consistency* of behavior, the *integration* and the *unity* of one's personality, and the *interdependence* of an individual's traits and dispositions are all keywords in Allport's writings, and they all necessitate the overarching principle of homeostasis.

Homeostasis likewise serves the basis of the theories and lifework of both Lewin (1936, 1964), and Heider (1958). Lewin's field theory of personality posits that whenever the human organism is thrown out of balance (by internal or external forces), self-regulatory processes will be initiated to restore balance. An unfinished task, for example, creates tension, which disappears when the task is completed through thinking or acting. Or consider the disequilibrium created by a serious disagreement with a friend. In most people this would set in motion one of several behavior sequences, aimed at reducing tension: break up the friendship, try to clarify the disagreement through a discussion, deny to oneself that there was a disagreement, enlist a mutual friend as a mediator, and so on. In all of these cases the ultimate goal is homeostasis, that is, the return of the individual to a state of equilibrium.

Heider's theory of cognitive consistency again assumes the constant operation of the ubiquitous homeostatic principle: Balance among one's cognitions is preferred to imbalance, for the latter is the source of unpleasant tension. Whenever a person encounters inconsistent cognitions, s/he will attempt to restore consistency by changing (and often distorting) one of the inconsistent elements. The famous "my enemy's enemy is my friend" adage is based on this homeostatic mechanism: if you discover that your enemy has an enemy, you can either like or dislike that person. Disliking this third party would create imbalance, for s/he, just like you, opposes your enemy. All you have to do in order to reduce or avoid the tension created by this imbalance is to regard him or her as your friend, and create the semblance of a coalition (see Moore, 1978). An analogous process often takes place within small groups, such as the family: A daughter takes her previously ignored father's side when he has a bitter argument with the brother she has always envied. (For the underlying concept of *triangulation*, see pp. 26–27, as well as Kramer-Moore and Moore, 2002, pp. 87–94.)

The need to apply this broadly accepted principle to family psychology was recognized about half a century ago by Don Jackson, one of the founding figures of family therapy. Jackson (1981) regarded the family as a "homeostatic unit," in which a change in one member is likely to be balanced by change(s) in other(s). Sometimes the recreation of homeostasis involves a simple see-saw action: as one person in the group weakens, another gains strength, or the increase in the psychological well-being of one is closely followed by the mental or physical breakdown of another. Jackson brings the following brief example: "A husband urged his wife into psychotherapy because of her frigidity. After several months of therapy she felt less sexually inhibited, whereupon the husband became impotent." What we observe here was aptly described by Gestalt theorists Perls, Hefferline, and Goodman (1973, p. 159) as the "slavish restoration of the status quo."

Satir, a strong proponent of the need to analyze communication patterns within the family, also found family homeostasis an indispensable concept: "the family acts so as to achieve a balance in relationships" (Satir, 1983, p. 1). She observed, just as Jackson had, that family groups exhibited an extremely potent tendency to restore balance, once it was disturbed, so that "other family members got worse as the patient got better" (Satir, 1983, p. 3). Notice the implications of this statement: the family, with its troubled member (the IP), is in a state of balance, which is disturbed by the success of therapy. Now the role of the IP is taken on by another family member, and balance is restored. By preventing healthy problem solving, all four of the dysfunctional communication patterns identified by Satir (blaming, placating, being super-rational, and being irrelevant; see pp. 74–75), and used by individuals in response to stress, act in the service of the homeostatic principle: they prolong the current troubled status of the family.

Yet, in spite of its apparent universality, homeostasis (aka negative feedback) does not account for the totality of human behavior. Indeed, most of the famous psychologists we have quoted realized that there was something wrong with regarding ourselves as subject to instincts "whose aim is to conduct the restlessness of life into the stability of the inorganic state" (Freud, 1961, p. 160). The very concept of development appears to be negated by the extreme conservatism of homeostasis. Neither can these death instincts, served by what Freud aptly referred to as "the Nirvana principle," account for the richness of the human experience, for creativity, curiosity and inventiveness.

A solution to this dilemma can be found in the dialectic conceptions of Altman, Vinsel, and Brown (1981), who regarded both complete stability and continuous change as maladaptive: "our dialectic perspective assumes that viable social bonds possess elements of both stability and change and of both openness and closedness, with either side of these opposites possibly stronger than the other at a given moment but with neither pole ever totally dominating. It is only with elements of each oppositional pole present, even to a minimal extent, that a relationship can grow, adapt, and respond to variations in internal and external circumstances" (p. 142).

We are in agreement with Altman et al.'s position: Both stagnation and frenzied change are signs of dysfunction in interpersonal relationships. (A similar opinion can be found in Clarkson and Mackewn, 1993, who wrote about "the polarities of homeostasis and disturbance" as well as in Olson, 2000, who included flexibility in his circumplex model of family functioning.) When frequently used within families, both extremes serve as examples of Family Defense Mechanisms (see Chapter 2, as well as Schwebel, 1993). The short-term gains most of them provide (mainly anxiety reduction) are more than offset by the long-term damage they cause: a total lack of stability creates a chaotic family, where the consistently unexpected behavior of members creates insurmountable obstacles for everyone. At the other extreme, strict homeostasis results in rigidity, and prevents the family from adjusting to the necessarily changing needs of its members.

Since traditions, customs, and the "wisdom of ages" all endorse the homeostatic half of the continuum, we shall counteract this trend by pointing out the particular dangers lying in some frequently heard sayings about "not rocking the boat." (For some religious doctrinal rejection of change see Moore and Kramer, 2000.) These myths and sayings, like those in subsequent chapters, are used in families, and are passed on from generation to generation to preserve the status quo. We shall show that by religiously preserving the current situation and by anxiously adhering to "better the devil you know," the sources of these sayings, instead of helping their partner/child/friend/relative cope, cause them pain and damage through stagnation.

The common element in all the following examples is the need to silence the speaker who dared to voice some pain caused by a family interaction or process. The unequal relationship, in which the silencer compels the speaker to shut up, stratifies the relationship, thus undermining equality and mutual respect. Ironically, at some later stage, this forced silence will not protect family members from what they are so afraid to hear; it will bring about the deterioration of the relationship: "communication cycles between members of the family will become more and more abbreviated until merely the raising of an eyebrow will trigger pain and rage in other family members" (Bandler, Grinder, and Satir, 1976, p. 108).

Any topic can be the grounds for disagreement (child rearing, home maintenance, extended family, friends, family history, previous affairs, substance abuse, intimacy, physical abuse past and present, etc.). Families having an open communication system are able to cope with their differences of opinion in a healthy, constructive manner. Those who have a closed system tend to become destructive and chaotic, making things worse as they encounter interpersonal difficulties. Both Bowen (1978) and Satir (1988) wrote extensively about open and closed communication. Satir describes a communication problem in families whose "rule is that one can talk about only the good, the right, the appropriate, and the relevant" (p. 119; see more on this in Box 5.1). Since reality is necessarily different from this ideal picture, family members will react by lying, concealing or just keeping mum.

Some couples, after years of evading painful issues, become strangers who can talk only about formal, "safe" topics. Intimacy is over in such closed relationships, and the constant censoring of their communication causes pain, alienation, and isolation (see Bowen, 1976b).

Restrictions on speech (a major characteristic of closed communication) are very costly to a family's mental health. Communication is blocked, intimacy is destroyed, with pseudo-mutuality often taking its place. In a pseudo-mutual family (see Chapter 2) the facade of "everything is okay" is used to hide conflict, while family members feel isolated and estranged from each other. The lack of openness in the system ensures that while members are alone in their pain and cannot ask or receive support from each other, they are also prevented from talking about "forbidden topics" to outsiders. The most common results are psychosomatic symptoms, depression, substance abuse, suicidal ideation, and either active or passive aggressiveness. None of the problems is dealt with and the ban on voicing the "unmentionables" prevents members from seeking much needed help.

There is a common myth underlying taboos and silences: trouble will disappear if it is not talked about. This unfounded and harmful belief is further nourished by frustration ("we've talked about this endlessly, and nothing has changed"), by embarrassment ("how could I have been so stupid as to get into this trouble"), by the need to avoid pain to oneself ("things are bad enough, why add to it by talking about it"), or to the other ("why should I involve you; I'll just suffer quietly").

The following utterances are all homeostatic communication blockers: They try to maintain the current situation by shutting up the person who threatens the status quo. Here, as well as in the following chapters, the setting is an informal, intimate dialogue, such as would take place within a family, or between two persons well acquainted with each other. (The same scenes are frequent also in the mass media, such as soap operas).

Let's not talk about it

Following what was perhaps a long hesitation, one member of the dyad has approached the other with a relationship problem. S/he may be in some distress, or has just felt a need to share some interpersonal event with a friend or a family member. Now the latter responds: Let's not talk about it. In the family, simple, direct and unmasked censorship is often expressed by such sentences, as I don't want to hear about it/Not everything has to be talked about/Too much talk has never really solved a problem.

There are several messages underlying these expressions:

1. I choose what we can talk about (safe topics for me), and what should be left unvoiced. (The source uses a control mechanism, establishes an authoritarian relationship, conveys a totalitarian frame of mind.)
2. If you want to talk about things that might be unpleasant to me, I'll turn a deaf ear. (Threat of isolation.)
3. In our relationship there is no room for talking about pain, sharing emotions other than positive and acceptable ones. (Demand for no intimacy and no authenticity, while presenting a pseudo-mutual façade.)
4. Talking is meaningless, a waste of time. (Lack of healthy, intimate communication, no option of working things out, a preference for closed communication and taboos.)
5. If we don't talk about our problems, they'll disappear; if we talk, they'll be amplified. (Childish empowerment of words, denial, repression, distortion of reality.)
6. If these words are not spoken, we can go on as if things never happened (denial, suppression), and we can forgive and forget. (A family myth which tends to create bitterness and hostility.)
7. Expressions of overt conflict are pathological; by not expressing them we prove ourselves to be a "good family." (Masking, inauthenticity, pseudo-mutuality.)
8. I have no skills of dealing with pain, disagreement, and differences of opinion, so these discussions make me feel stupid and useless. (Self-preservation by suppressing the other.)

Clearly, the suppressors of family communication hope to gain some peace of mind, as well as to maintain a semblance of the "good relationship." They enforce boundaries for communication to serve their own needs, against the speaker's wishes. When the silencing occurs between spouses, we can expect a deterioration of intimacy in the relationship, a growing distance, less and less open communication, secretiveness and isolation. When it occurs between parents and children, the results are far reaching for the next generation, as well. The children will learn not to confide in their parents, and instead of communicating thoughts and feelings, they will be more likely to act out on them. Children will learn from their parental role model that intimate relationships are non-egalitarian, so one must always try to have the upper hand in order to dictate the rules. These children will be barred from developing healthy communication skills (both listening and expressing themselves authentically and with empathy), and will also demand the right to listen only to selected topics, to repress negative thoughts and feelings and expect others to do the same, to avoid sharing of inner world, to use pathogenic communication patterns with their future spouses and children, and so to pass this on from one generation to the next.

An extreme form of "not talking about it" is the keeping of secrets within the family. A few aspects of this PFP are discussed in Box 5.1.

Box 5.1 Family secrets

> . . . if I hear a parent getting hysterical about something her or his child is doing, I look immediately to see whether the child's behavior has stirred up a secret in the parent's youth (Satir, 1988, p. 127).

Bowen (1976b, pp. 335–336) distinguished between open and closed relationship systems. In a healthy, open system individual members of an intimate group, such as the family, feel free to share many of their thoughts and feelings. Other members of the group, with whom these inner contents of one's life are shared, are likewise free to reciprocate. Such sharing may take place both within and between generations: there is openness – though not necessarily to the same degree – between two adults, between two children, as well as between an adult and a child. Closed systems abound in secrets and taboos: parents keep secrets from their children and from each other; children do not feel free to confide their thoughts to their parents. While people often claim that they avoid talking about some subjects in order to protect the other person, Bowen suggested that their motivation is to protect themselves from the anxiety their communication is likely to create in the other: "If people could follow intellectual knowledge instead of the automatic reflex [of protecting themselves], and they could gain some control over their own reactiveness to anxiety in the other, they would be able to talk about taboo subjects in spite of the anxiety, and the relationship would move toward a more healthy openness."

Everyone has problems!

Think of a young woman who comes to her parents (or it could be her sister or best friend) to complain about her marriage: "I'm unhappy," she says, "I want to leave him!" In the true spirit of homeostasis they reply: "Everyone has problems!" Or they might say, "No marriage is perfect!" "Imagine what would happen if everyone just got up and left, because things weren't wonderful!" Another possible response: "No one promised you a bed of roses. We stayed together, even though things were far from perfect for us."

When the complaint is more specific, so is the common response: You should've known that men can't be trusted! Boys will be boys! You think you're the only one whose husband cheats/drinks/gambles?

All of these responses have the same underlying messages in common:

1. Stay in your marriage. (Involves denial and control on the part of the source of the utterance, and demands repression from its target.)
2. Compromise and don't expect to be happy. (Stagnation and a demand to stop hoping for anything better.)
3. Stop complaining. (Repression, control, and an announcement of the lack of support.)

Who benefits from this response? Apparently, not the young, unhappy woman. None of these responses help her, for they offer no hope and emphasize her loneliness and the deprivation of her right to strive for some improvement in her quality of life. Instead of empathizing with her, and supporting her in reaching a healthy coping option as a solution to her problem, they all support the impasse she is in. The only beneficiaries are the parents. By sticking to their policy of "no change," they are attempting to control the complainer and are actively maintaining a dysfunctional situation. There is nothing mysterious about their motivation: If she leaves him, who will support her? Will she want to move back with us? What about the children? Will we have to take care of them when she is at work? They may be also validating their own history of remaining in an unhappy marriage. Their response reflects *their* needs, not hers.

We may assume that before approaching her parents, the young wife tried to talk to her husband, and more than likely she received a similar reaction. Being told, again and again, that e*veryone has problems*, creates a wall between her and all the meaningful people who were supposed to be on her side. If homeostasis prevails, it will be due to the lack of social support, and not to her situation having become more bearable.

The same reactions that maintain unhealthy homeostasis are typical in parent-child relationships: A child complains of having a rough time at school. One of his parents says: "Everyone has problems! Do you think I enjoy going to work every day? Life is not just fun and games!" Clearly, this response will not make the child happier at school, but might make it decide not to share future agonies with its parents. As in the previous example, the parents hope to gain some peace of mind, by convincing the child that no matter what, it must stay in the current situation. By controlling the child's behavior, while ignoring its emotional plea, the parents try to enforce the status quo, without addressing the problem, for which they have no ready-made solution. They are motivated by the need to conform to social expectations (clearly *their* need, not the child's) and avoid coping with an unfamiliar situation (I don't know what to do if s/he leaves school). Putting their needs ahead of the child's is typical of situations that revolve around the overarching theme of homeostasis.

Count your blessings

Another form of creating homeostasis is by not only ignoring the stated pain and frustration of family members who have chosen to confide, but even putting a heavier load on them by demanding an "optimistic approach," which has no relevant bearing on the situation.

In this case, common reactions to the predicament of the above wife or child would be: *Things could be much worse! Look at the bright side: At least you've got your health! Be happy that he doesn't drink, or beat you/she's good to the children/ you've a roof over your head. Other children would love to trade places with you. You don't know how lucky you are . . .* A very effective threat can be added to these "cheerful" reminders: *By rocking the boat you could lose what you have.* Or: *One day you'll learn what unhappy truly means.*

When looked at more closely, these seemingly optimistic statements are desperately pessimistic. The unhappy child or spouse gets the following underlying messages:

1. You are lucky (and undeserving) to have even this much. (Undermines self-worth.)
2. One should repress negative feelings and never share them even with close people. (Repression and isolation.)

3. Shared feelings will be trampled. (Oppression, creates distance and lack of trust.)
4. There is always worse to fear and nothing better to hope and strive for. (Threat of revenge.)
5. I'm not interested in anything but my own comfort level. (An indifferent and self-centred world.)
6. I know more about life than you do. (Lowers self-esteem, one-upmanship.)
7. If there is no comfort to be gained from sharing, and the result is feeling even more guilty and worthless, it is better to shut up. (Control and isolation.)
8. Compromise, compromise, compromise, even if this means giving up all your dreams and living a miserable life. (Depressing.)

So let us examine again: Who benefits from these remarks? It is again the sender of the message rather than its receiver. Indeed, responding to the other's plight with a cliché is much less demanding than delving into the source of the pain and dealing with it. Delivering these empty messages takes a few seconds, and the illusion of having solved the problem can be kept up, while facing the need for change and implementing it, take time and energy. The person is left with the same pain (another instance of homeostasis), with an added feeling of loneliness and guilt.

If this exchange takes place between spouses, it is an effective method of shunning responsibility, of avoiding painful insight to one's deficiencies, while maintaining control through shutting up the other. In preventing a spouse from talking about difficulties, the hidden threat is that the spouse could lose even the little peace of mind there is. By implying "be glad I don't drink, or beat you" there is a not too subtle threat that things can become much worse, so one must collaborate with the pathogenic relationship.

The same holds for parent/child interactions. The parent says this to the child who feels neglected, repressed, discriminated against. Now the child is accused of being ungrateful, pessimistic, constantly dissatisfied. S/he is also asked to join the myth of "we're a good family, and as far as families go, there is nothing better to hope and work for." The only one who gains (and only in the short term, for the temporary quiet will be paid for by more severe disturbance) is the parent, interested in sustaining the status quo, without examining the underlying family dynamics and their consequences.

Better the devil you know

The need for security creates a preference for homeostasis. Changes are threatening, so people put up with painful situations for extended periods of time. An extreme, though far from rare, example concerns marital violence: on average women attempt to leave an abusive relationship seven times before they finally succeed (Domestic Violence Victimization, 1998). There are many reasons for this: abused spouses may feel they deserve their fate; they can't believe anything better will come their way; often they are ashamed to divulge what they are going through as if it was their fault; they may also be afraid of more severe consequences if they try to break free. Low self-esteem and a fear of the unknown play a dominant role in this stagnation, making it very difficult for therapists and social workers to help abuse victims break free.

So imagine that either the abuse victim or a person in a less tragic position says to his or her confidant: "I've decided to leave/I'm fed up with my job/This relationship is not going anywhere/I'm going to move out of this dingy flat!" – The latter responds by throwing a bucket of ice-cold water: "Why don't you stick to the old and tried?" "Don't you know that this is as good as it gets?" "Don't make waves!" "Don't stick your neck out!" "Better the devil you know."

Let us examine the messages underlying such responses.

1. Changes are bad, dangerous and the outcome is even more painful. (Homeostasis in its purest and most direct form, through threat of worse things to come.)
2. You don't have it in you to improve your life, so better stick with the curse that you are familiar with; at least it won't tax your coping skills that aren't great. (Belittling the talker.)
3. Our lot is suffering; we all deserve what we get. (Despair, demand to resign oneself to being a victim, self-blaming.)
4. I've learned the hard way that things get only worse. If I couldn't get myself a better life and have put up with the bad, you won't either. (Self-justification at the other's expense, distorting the other's reality, and ruining their chances for a better life.)

In all of these responses the speaker admits that things are bad, but at the same time, sends a message of hopelessness and despair for anything better. A common thread running through all the sayings we have encountered is their self-serving character. Those who themselves have not made changes, would feel even more miserable and have an even lower self-esteem, if they saw others being able to move on; so they have a personal interest in seeing others fail to improve their lives. These speakers are overwhelmed by fear and anxiety, so they project their fear onto others, and try to validate their own inability to do better for themselves. At the same time, the person who, though hesitant, is on the verge of making a life-changing decision, is denied emotional support. This is more than mere disappointment: the outcome of this dialogue can only be a betrayal of confidence and of trust in the present, and a danger of estrangement in the future. When the exchange is between parents and children, it is more than likely that transgenerational learning will take place: it is through such experiences that homeostatic messages are passed from one generation to the other and keep individuals locked in misery.

Before leaving the topic of homeostasis, we must emphasize: we do not advocate change for the sake of change. Though in the above analyses we have been critical of several homeostasis promoting sayings, we can empathize with parents, spouses or friends who prefer constancy to variation, and who advise their significant others to act likewise. In addition to projecting their own anxiety (probably acquired in similar situations, where they were on the receiving end of advice), they are also worried about the other person's assumed lack of ability to cope with difficulties: "Is she oversensitive?" "Is he just spoiled?" "Will she ruin her marriage for a petty reason?" Our censoring these fears and anxieties would be as unhealthy as silencing the complainer. Both the listener and the therapist face a dilemma. On the one hand, it is important to put across the message that frustrating relationships in one's life can many times be worked at, and that both parties have to make some effort to improve them. On the other hand, every complainer has probably hesitated for a long time before mustering the courage to both complain and try to make an essential change in his/her life; any homeostatic message might stilt this growth. What is needed here, as well as in the case of all the dysfunctional sayings that appear in the following chapters, is an alternative, *congruent* response. The latter is neither encouraging the hasty breaking up of relationships nor the stubborn sticking to one's guns, but rather the use of healthy communication patterns, which have a better chance to empower both speaker and listener, to strengthen intimacy, and to result in either lasting and improved relationships or clearly seeing the options and making better choices for all of them.

Here are two examples of congruent communication. Let us look again at the young woman who comes to her parents (or another intimate friend or family member) to complain about her marriage: "I'm unhappy," she says, "I want to leave him!" A congruent reply would run along these lines:

"I'm sorry to hear that you are unhappy in your marriage. To be honest, my first reaction is anxiety, because I have always been so afraid of taking big steps in my own life. But the last thing I want is for you to be unhappy, so could we examine the problem and the possible options, together?" This reply is honest about the difficulty the listener feels, but is respectful of the speaker, and invites teamwork at trying to cope, instead of turning against the speaker or the possibility of a change. It is not based on clichés, promises to listen from a perspective that gives first priority to the speaker's well being, and is open to any solution.

We shall also suggest a congruent response to the child who complained of having a rough time at school: "It must be very hard to go to school every morning when you have a rough time there. I wonder if you can tell me more about it, so we can either think of how to cope better and make school more bearable for you, or we might need to ask for some help. I have no readymade answers, but I want to stand by you, so I'd like to have a fuller picture of what's going on." In this case, too, the well-being of the child is uppermost, and s/he is not left alone to deal with the problem. There is no promise of an easy solution or an immediate one, nor does the parent pose as one who knows everything and is able to solve any problem. The child gains from having confided in the parent, because s/he feels that the parent cares and will share shouldering the problem and the search for some solution.

In neither of these replies have the listeners enforced silence through a stereotypical homeostatic reply, or turned their back on the confiding person. There are no shortcuts: the listeners will act as supporting agents in the (sometimes) long process of making a desired change. In reality, family members usually want to be loving and supportive, but they do not know how, and are overcome by their own anxiety and biases. It is the counselor or therapist who should act as a "teacher" (Satir, 1983, p. 129) and teach family members how to use congruent communication patterns. In order to do this, therapists and counselors must themselves be congruent.

Activities

1 A word to the wise

Trigger: Choose a saying from this chapter (or use one of your own) that is pertinent to this family. Alternatively, prepare a poster with several appropriate sayings and ask the family to select one that they find all too familiar to them. Ask each family member to write and read out to the others a very short script, describing a family event where this saying would be used by one of them.

Possible points for discussion:

What are the costs and benefits of this saying?
Who gains and who loses by it?
Under what circumstances is it used?
What lies behind it, what does it cover up?
What anxieties are involved?
How does it hurt the listener?
Which dysfunctional communication pattern does it illustrate? (see pp. 74–75).

Now ask each to substitute a congruent, authentic, empathic I-message (see p. 75) for the saying used earlier. (This activity can be repeated, using other appropriate sayings).

2 Action blockers

Trigger: Family members sit in a circle, in a darkened room. Close your eyes and think of words or sentences that stop you from making meaningful changes in your life. [pause] Now open your eyes, say these words and sentences aloud, and I'll write them on this board.

Classify the results into groups according to common agendas and themes. Who says these words (for each group of expressions)? Let's examine together what is the overt motivation of the speaker, and what could be the covert (underlying, hidden) motivation? Write these on the board. How do you feel when you look at these explanations? Discuss your feelings with the others. End the session by voluntary sharing.

When you leave this session, think about an occasion when you tried to stop a member of your family from making a meaningful change in his or her life. Look at your motivation and think about the effect your words had on this person's life.

3 Time travel

This is a guided imagination activity.

Trigger: Darken the room, speak slowly, in a relaxed, low voice: Sit in a comfortable position, close your eyes, breathe deeply. Travel back in time to your childhood. Think about a family event during your childhood which made you very unhappy and that you wanted to change but couldn't. Look at yourself and at those around you, at that time. What made you so unhappy? Who made it impossible for you to make the change and how? What are the words that stopped you from acting? [pause] The next stop in your time travel is during your adolescence or early adulthood. Think again about something you wanted to change but were prevented from doing. What are the words that stopped you from acting? Who could have said them? [pause] Breathe deeply, move your limbs, open your eyes slowly. Turn on the lights.

Possible points for discussion:

Look at yourself in the present time. What would you like to change now, and what stops you from making this change?
What is the common factor to the voices preventing the change?
What do you gain and what do you lose by giving in to these voices?
Share the feelings that you've experienced during this activity.

End the session with the following request: You have now been through a personal experience, and were invited to listen to the experience of other family members. What insights do you take from this meeting?

4 A note to myself

Trigger: Jot down a significant change in your life that you have wished for, but couldn't bring about. [pause] Put the note in an envelope and seal it. Consider the forces that push you forward, and those that prevent you from making this change. Evidently, the forces pulling you back have been stronger.

In the family circle: Discuss the difficulties in making this significant change, without revealing its exact nature. Think of the individuals involved in this conflict. What are their overt and covert messages? [pause] Close your eyes. Imagine that you open this envelope in five years time, and realize that you still haven't made this wished for change. What will you tell yourself then? End the session with voluntary sharing.

5 Script writing

Trigger: Present family members with one of the situations in this chapter, using the homeostatic sayings appearing there. Alternatively, ask them to write a short dialogue based on their own life, involving a homeostatic event.

Discuss each dialogue and the underlying messages and motivations of the speakers. [pause] Choose one of the dialogues and "translate" it into a congruent alternative. What were the difficulties you've experienced when translating the dialogue? End the session with voluntary sharing.

6

Lack of Authenticity, or Keep a Stiff Upper Lip

This above all – to thine own self be true,
And it must follow, as the night the day,
Thou canst not then be false to any man. (Shakespeare, *Hamlet* I: iii)

Polonius may not have been the wisest of men, yet his fatherly advice to Laertes is worth considering. What lies behind this advice is *authenticity*.

Destructive Myths in Family Therapy: How to Overcome Barriers to Communication by Seeing and Saying – A Humanistic Perspective, First Edition. Daniela Kramer-Moore and Michael Moore.
© 2012 John Wiley & Sons, Ltd. Published 2012 by John Wiley & Sons, Ltd.

We realize, along with such social critics and thinkers as Trilling (1972) and Taylor (1991) that the desirability of authenticity is not without controversy. Along with other basic tenets we subscribe to (such as democracy, equality, individualism, and self-actualization) it has been criticized on social and political grounds, and yet we regard it not just as another useful trait, but as an ideal that must be pursued for the sake of mental health.

We will now look at four modern psychological versions of Polonius' counsel: the rejection of automaton conformity, the pursuit of genuineness, developing of the solid self, and the search for congruence in communication.

Four Conceptions of Authenticity

Though the first two theorists we shall consider, Erich Fromm and Carl Rogers, do not belong to the circle of family therapists, they played an important role in the development of this field in general, and in the recognition of the centrality of authenticity, in particular.

Fromm (1965) described the price modern men pay for the increasing freedoms they have gained: isolation, alienation, bewilderment, anxiety. To escape from these, and thus to escape from freedom, various defense mechanisms are used; one of them is *automaton conformity*:

> the individual ceases to be himself; he adopts entirely the kind of personality offered to him by cultural patterns; and he therefore becomes exactly as all others are and as they expect him to be (p. 208).

Fromm found that such conformity forms the basis of people's blind submission to authority. Instead of taking responsibility for their thoughts and acts, they let some external power (such as religious or political ideology) take control of their lives. Many of Fromm's democratic and humanistic values, summarized in his "Credo" (1962, pp. 174–182), are echoed throughout this book: that life means constant change, that we cannot make choices for others, and that therapists, counselors or teachers are effective only if they are authentic and practice what they preach. His fight against "the deathly grip of clichés" in broader society is analogous to our efforts to show the threat certain myths pose to the mental health and well-being of families.

Conformity is related to another important personality variable: the locus of control of reinforcement. Introduced into psychology nearly half a century ago by Julian Rotter (an American psychologist who studied under Kurt Lewin) this trait represents the degree to which individuals believe that they can control the rewards they receive in life. Those who have an internal locus of control believe that whatever happens to them is primarily a result of their own behavior. At the other end of the continuum we find those with an external locus of control: they believe that external forces, mainly luck, fate, and other people, control their lives. Whether a person feels internally or externally controlled has important behavioral consequences: the former are better, for example, at setting and achieving goals, and at coping with stressful situations (see Wang, Bowling, and Eschleman, 2010). Several studies, among them one by Avtgis (1998), made the inevitable connection between conformity and locus of control, finding that those whose scores indicate an external locus of control are more easily persuaded, are less able to resist social influence and conform more than their internally controlled counterparts.

The type of conformity discussed by Fromm is only one of a wide range of related social psychological constructs (see Box 6.1).

Box 6.1 Types of conformity

How do people influence others' behavior? What makes some of us submit to social pressure? Social psychologists have given a lot of thought to the pervasive phenomenon of conformity.

Herbert Kelman (1958) made an important contribution by identifying three major types of social influence: In *compliance* a person publicly submits to another's will in order to either gain some benefit ("If you're nice to grandma, I'll let you stay up late") or to avoid some harm ("Stop whining or I'll hit you!"). As a rule (though there may be exceptions), such behaviors persist only as long as the source of the influence is present; therefore compliance is only skin deep.

Identification is based on the attractiveness of the source. Many of us dress, speak, or behave similarly to people we admire and respect; we even tend to adopt their attitudes and opinions. Conformity achieved through identification goes deeper than compliance, yet its duration is also conditional: it lasts only as long as the source remains attractive.

(continued)

Internalization is the deepest and most enduring form of social impact: it occurs when one receives the answer to a very important question, when a person learns from a highly reliable source what s/he considers to be "the truth" (cf. "informational dependence" in Jones and Gerard, 1967, pp. 78–79). The family myths encountered in this book, delivered by all-knowing parents to their thirsty-for-knowledge children are internalized, and therefore quite resistant to change.

Hollander (1981, pp. 220–221) drew a distinction between two types of conformity: *consistency* and *movement*. In the former people automatically adopt the norms and customs of their social circle. Their behavior is not unlike automaton conformity, described above by Fromm. In the family context we constantly see children unquestioningly accepting family truths, regardless of their validity; an extreme example of this is a child rejecting medical treatment on religious grounds. A measure of consistency conformity is necessary for the continued existence of any group, including that of families, but group members should be encouraged to occasionally stop and reflect: What makes me behave like this? What are the costs and benefits of my behavior? Do I have an alternative?

Movement conformity is described by Hollander as "a shift of response to a socially prescribed standard from an individual's preferred judgment." Such conforming behavior is similar to compliance, one of the three types of social influence described above by Kelman; a common example is a child yielding to peer pressure and acting against his or her better judgment so as to avoid being ostracized.

A further significant addition to the conceptualization of conformity was made by Willis, whose bi-dimensional diamond model is described in Nail and Van Leeuwen (1993). The first dimension of this model ranges from total conformity (this could be a placating child who submits to a parent's every demand) to total anticonformity (this is illustrated by the rebellious teenager who does the opposite of what the parent wants). Behaviors falling at either of these points cannot be authentic, for they are dictated by, and predictable from, the wishes of another. The second dimension, orthogonal to the first, ranges between independence and variability. Neither of these behaviors is

(continued)

predictable, though only the former one can possibly be authentic: independent individuals make up their own minds – going along with the wishes of others if such behavior is in accordance with their needs, and opposing them if it does not. At the other end of this dimension lies variability or self-anticonformity, where a person's behavior is inconsistent. This is a potentially pathological pattern, related to low self-esteem.

Carl Rogers (1980; see also his publications 1967, 1990a, 1990b, 1990c) used interchangeably several terms that partially overlap with authenticity: *genuineness, congruence, realness*, and *transparence*. All of these words have to do with a matching of experience, awareness, and communication, a person's internal consistency and acceptance of self, the lack of facades, roles, pretences, or defenses. These characteristics equally apply to therapist/counselor and client; indeed, without therapists being genuine, one cannot expect their clients to move in the same direction. Rogers describes three conditions for the "therapeutic movement to ensue"; these are "the therapist's congruence or genuineness; unconditional positive regard, [also known as] a complete acceptance; and a sensitively accurate empathic understanding" (1990a, p. 11). The therapeutic process involves a continuum from incongruence to congruence, for throughout it the client becomes "more acceptant of himself, he also moves toward greater congruence, he finds it possible to move out from behind the facades he has used, to drop his defensive behaviors, and more openly to be what he truly is" (Rogers, 1967, p. 64). Rogers employed the concept of congruence also in his description of the self: During therapy the gap between the client's perception of reality, actual self, and ideal self is reduced, both because self-regard turns more positive, and ideal self becomes more realistic (1990c, p. 242). A further aspect necessarily concerns parent – child relationships: To be able to experience unconditional positive regard toward one's children and to show them empathy, parents need to be congruent and have unconditional self-regard (1990c, p. 253).

Congruence can be operationalized, and its essence made more tangible, through the use of the Q-Sort technique. Individuals are asked to sort a large set of self-descriptive statements (such as "very outgoing and social", "organized and detail oriented", or "I am an aggressive person") into a number of piles (typically nine). The latter are arranged along a continuum ranging from "least like me" to "most like me" (see a detailed example of this ranking procedure in Carducci, 2009, pp. 221–224). To measure congruence, individuals sort the statements twice: once to describe how they perceive themselves now (their actual self), and then how they would like to be (ideal self). The more similar the two sorts are (as expressed by a rank-order correlation coefficient), the more congruent is the person performing the sorting. Rogers suggested that Q-Sorts be used also for measuring changes in clients' self-perception that occur during therapy, or for the investigation of how therapists see the relationship between themselves and their client.

Both Murray Bowen and Virginia Satir, whose approaches to authenticity we shall consider next, are among the leading figures of the family therapy movement.

Bowen (1976a) developed a theory in which the *solid*, as opposed to the *pseudo-self*, plays an important role. One's solid self is independent of social pressures, proclaiming "This is what I am, what I believe, what I stand for, and what I will do or will not do" (p. 68). The solid self's beliefs and opinions are the result of reflection on one's life experience, and are arrived at after careful consideration of several alternatives. Having made a choice among these alternatives, the individual with a solid self feels responsible for the consequences. The pseudo-self, echoing Fromm's automaton conformist, is an inauthentic "pretend" self, often containing the views and principles of conflicting sources, with a chameleon-like tendency to fit itself to the immediate pressures of other persons and situations. When a person is in a situation that creates high anxiety, those with a solid self are able to take action, while in the pseudo-self emotional and intellectual functioning become fused, leading to emotion-flooded, dysfunctional behavior.

In addition to the four dysfunctional communication patterns described by Satir (see pp. 74–75, above), she also recognized a healthy, *congruent* pattern. Congruent communicators are not manipulative, share their thoughts and emotions about themselves without projecting them onto others, and minimize the gap between words and intentions. Satir's (1988, pp. 369–370) depiction of congruent living in Box 6.2 is a utopia well worth striving for!

Congruent communication consists of both listening and responding. Satir (1988, p. 71) described a good listener as one who gives full attention to the speaker and is fully present; puts aside any preconceived ideas of what the speaker is going to say; interprets what is going on descriptively and not judgmentally; is alert for any confusion and asks questions to get clarity; lets the speaker know that the speaker has been heard and also the content of what was communicated.

Box 6.2 The essentials of congruent living

To communicate clearly.
To cooperate rather than compete.
To empower rather than subjugate.
To enhance individual uniqueness rather than categorize.
To use authority to guide and accomplish "what fits" rather than force
    compliance through the tyranny of power.
To love, value, and respect themselves fully.
To be personally and socially responsible.
To use problems as challenges and opportunities for creative solutions.

(Satir, 1988, pp. 369–370)

Authenticity as a Trait

Recently all of these ideas – Fromm's rejection of automaton conformity, Bowen's solid self, Satir's search for congruence, Rogers' placing genuineness at the very centre of the therapeutic process – have received renewed attention by the positive psychology movement. The founder of that movement, Martin Seligman (2002), described it as follows: "Psychology is not just about illness or health; it also is about work, education, insight, love, growth, and play. . . positive psychology does not rely on wishful thinking, self-deception, or hand waving; instead it tries to adopt what is best in the scientific method to the unique problems that human behaviour presents in all its complexity." In this spirit, an overarching term, *authenticity*, has been suggested to cover the various aspects of what the above theorists and therapists value so much (Harter, 2002). Wood et al. (2008) developed a scale for its measurement. Unlike the Q-Sort, whose results pertain to an individual, and permit only intrapersonal comparisons, the Authenticity Scale is a measure of a trait or disposition that allows interpersonal analyses.

Wood et al. (2008) derived their definition of authenticity from a Rogerian, person-centered approach. Here it is assumed that the three levels of experiencing – primary/physiological states, conscious awareness of these states, and their outward expression through verbal and non-verbal behaviors – can be matched or mismatched. While perfect congruence between actual awareness and its symbolic representation in consciousness is never attainable, its extent is one aspect of authenticity. When one feels "out of touch" with one's true self, lack of authenticity and self-alienation occur. Another aspect of authenticity concerns the relationship between conscious awareness and outward expression. Wood et al. referred to the match between these two levels of experiencing as authentic living (cf. Satir's congruent living, mentioned earlier). One leads an authentic life if one lives in accordance with one's values and beliefs. (Though it is necessary to add that one's authentic living must neither be forced on others nor harm them in any way). The final aspect of authenticity concerns the degree to which a person is subject to the opinion of others. Similarly to Fromm's avowal of independence as opposed to automaton conformity, Wood et al. suggested that introjecting others' views leads to inauthenticity. Their conception of authenticity is well supported by empirical research: individuals who accept external influence in close relationships report lower self-esteem and more repression; those who report more variability between roles (i.e. they feel that their personality varies between the roles they take on) feel themselves less authentic; each of the three aspects of authenticity, as measured by the Authenticity Scale, is strongly related to self-esteem.

Pseudo Living

Ignoring Polonius' advice – "to thine own self be true" – leads to the creation of a pseudo-self. Bowen (1976a, pp. 68–69) suggested that individuals acquire a pseudo-self in order to conform to their social environment, or, as he puts it, "at the behest of the relationship system." The application of this notion to the system itself – that is, the family – lead Wynne et al. (1958) to coin the term *pseudo-mutuality* (along with enmeshment and disengagement, pseudo-mutuality is one of the three major examples of structural distortions; it is briefly discussed in Chapter 2).

A distinct characteristic of pseudo-mutuality is the insistence on its own desirability. The myth of "We are such a good family!" (see Chapter 2), along with several others to be discussed in this chapter, provides the family with the ideological basis of their distorted structure. Its core resembles the essence of homeostatic messages: change is to be avoided at all cost. While the myths of the previous chapter achieved this by serving as homeostatic communication blockers, the ones we shall look at now emphasize the need to maintain the fixed family role structure. The five sayings we shall analyze are but a small sample of a practically endless list of social dos and don'ts that contribute to the lack of authenticity: *always be polite; don't wear your heart on your sleeve; always appear successful; don't be a sore loser.* Parents and spouses convey the Layer B subtext: *don't worry me, so I can keep feeling good; let's pretend everything is ok.* Intimacy always involves authenticity, but at times it is painful and/or stressful. In order to avoid pain, some family members prefer distance to intimacy.

And They Lived Happily Ever After

Bedtime stories, told by parents to their children, often end on this note: having overcome considerable difficulties, the young couple marries and they live happily ever after. But it is not only old-fashioned fairy tales that leave their readers with an idyllic picture of marital bliss. The romantic fiction industry assures its vast market of the same happy ending. (Harlequin Books, one of 19 publishers of romantic fiction, sells about 175 million copies annually, in 24 languages, to at least 50 million readers; see Kramer and Moore, 2001a, 2001b). Neither is this myth limited to one culture: Metz (2007) described its appearance in societies as different from each other as Spain and India (in Telenova soap operas and Bollywood movies, respectively). This powerful myth idealizes marriage by offering an unfulfillable promise: no matter how many problems they have, regardless of how unsuitable they are, when two deserving persons fall in love, their difficulties magically disappear after the wedding. Yet Hollywood-type endings notwithstanding (from *Sleeping Beauty* to *Pretty Woman*), reality is very different. Not only does a large proportion of marriages end in divorce (40 to 50 percent in both the United Kingdom and the United States), but there is no reason to believe that those who remain in their marriage live happily ever after, either. A recent finding of a UK survey (Ermisch, Iacovou, and Skew, 2011) shows that for both men and women, happiness declines with the duration of the relationship, with the decline being steeper for women.

So at best, an individual, as part of a couple, has a good spousehood as a result of the effort invested in it, and not due to some magical quality inherent in the premarital stage. At worst, the spouse who refuses divorce or separation murders the one who wants out. In-between these two extremes there are all those children who witness their parents' incessant bickering, their covert and overt power struggles, and sometimes whispered, sometimes loudly proclaimed dissatisfaction with marriage. In their turn, these children are likely to copy their parents' behavior in and attitudes toward marriage when they reach adulthood.

Let us examine some possible motivations behind the myth of happy endings, in general, and of happy married life, in particular.

1. Escape: let's forget about our miserable life at least for the duration of reading, listening to, or watching a happy story. Let's hope there is something better than what we have now.
2. Encourage marriage: various social institutions, among them political and religious ones, perennially proclaim an interest in marriage, for social, moral, legal, or economic reasons.
3. Not only the social institutions, but most parents, as well, want to see their children happily married, both out of a genuine (though perhaps misguided) interest in the children's well-being, and out of simple self-interest.
4. These parents also need a confirmation of their own marriage, and would like to see their children follow in their footsteps.
5. The parents do not believe that true happiness can happen in reality; rather, it is found only in fairy tales and in magic. Their spreading of the myth of happy endings has a Layer C meaning, described in Chapter 1. The source of the message is blind to its deeper, hidden significance; nevertheless the listener can pick it up and be influenced by it.

Given current and projected divorce rates (Martin and Bumpass, 1989, estimated that within a few decades two-thirds of first marriages will end in divorce or separation) the promise of "happily ever after" is not just empty, it is also irresponsible. More generally, messages suggesting that positive outcomes will be gained without conscious effort ("Everything will be OK") are unhealthy.

C'mon, Give Daddy a Smile!

All newborns are authentic: They cry when uncomfortable, smile and gurgle when pleased, hit out when angered. The long process of socialization teaches them to consider their surroundings by not showing and not acting upon their true emotions. There is a thin line demarcating sublimation from suppression. When parents say "Don't hit!", they dictate behavior. When they say "Don't worry!" or "No reason to feel sad!", they attempt to control emotions. When it comes to "Be nice to Mommy (or sister, brother, etc.)!", they are encouraging a pseudo-self, the putting on of a mask: "Your emotions and the way you express them are unacceptable or threatening. You'd better learn to appease your surroundings, so give us a smile!" (See Bowen's approach, above). It can start with "Give Grandpa a kiss!" when the child has no such inclination whatsoever. Then, when the child falls and hurts its knee: "Don't cry, it's nothing!" The individual is taught to hide feelings, to express something else, to create a gap between inner world and outside expression, perhaps even to resort to reaction formation (a Freudian defense mechanism, described in Chapter 2). Eventually s/he may learn not to feel, so as to close the gap. Rape victims often report numbness or a need to avoid physical contact. The above saying is also a kind of rape: Smile when you're sad!

The source of such sayings may have several agendas:

1. One's own comfort. "I don't want to see sad faces around me; they remind me of my own troubles."
2. The other's comfort. Many believe that forcing positive thinking on others will bring about a genuine, lasting change. Instead, the listener is likely to feel isolated, misunderstood ("My feelings are disregarded"), or even guilty ("I shouldn't feel the way I do").
3. Social norms. Most societies frown upon the demonstration of certain emotions (be it anger, affection, or fear); the source wants to be disassociated from someone who violates these norms.
4. A fear of consequences. The listener's feelings must be reined in, lest the source loses control: "Will this get out of hand? Will I have to do anything?"

In his description of the attainment of autonomy, Berne (1964, pp. 182–183), wrote about how parents, "deliberately or unaware, teach their children from birth how to behave, think, feel and perceive." Liberation from these influences is essential for the autonomous person, one who is capable of awareness, spontaneity, and intimacy.

Awareness is "the capacity to see a coffeepot and hear the birds sing in one's own way, and not the way one was taught . . . Spontaneity means option, the freedom to choose and express one's feelings . . . Intimacy means the spontaneous, game-free candidness of an aware person" (Berne, 1964, pp. 178–180). Though he used a different set of terms, Berne's description of the autonomous person has a lot in common with the four conceptions of authenticity we encountered earlier in this chapter.

Play Hard to Get

The idea behind this saying is taken from the world of business and obeys the laws of supply and demand. If the merchant seems too eager to sell, the buyer may become suspicious: "Are the goods damaged? Have I offered too much?" However, if the seller appears reluctant, the message is: "My goods are worth a lot, I've other prospective buyers for them, so raise your offer!" Similar considerations apply to matchmakers in cultures where arranged marriages are customary. Within the family, this adage is more often than not aimed at women and has clear sexual connotations. A woman who is eager to have sex is considered "cheap." (This is an outstanding example of sexual double standards, for men's interest in sex is accepted or even expected.) When a daughter complies with the message, and plays hard to get, she is in effect saying: "I'm expensive goods. By giving myself to you, I'm doing you a favor!"

Letting the standards of public life enter and dictate the nature of personal relationships is always a dangerous practice. The commercialization of intimate interactions, lying at the bottom of *playing hard to get*, is likely to have serious consequences. If the bargain is consummated, there is more to come in the future. "I could have married Joe (who is richer), Bill (who is better looking), or Sam (who comes from a better family). So you owe me!" Another version, applicable to both genders, is keeping one's spouse at arm's length within the marriage. "Don't wear your heart on your sleeve!" is but a paraphrase of the above. If you express your emotions, reveal your need for your spouse, you lose your bargaining position. Saying "I love you", "I need you", "Hug me" might be interpreted as a sign of weakness, and might be used against you in the future. These bookkeeping notions turn spousehood into a continuous business transaction, where gaps between covert feelings and overt behavior are a routine matter. Haggling has taken the place of intimacy, and both partners must constantly be on guard for fear of being exploited.

This picture is frequently seen in family therapy: both partners hide their feelings for fear of being taken advantage of. One of the most important tasks of the therapist is to teach them to mean what they say and to say what they mean. Authenticity – possibly not the best policy in business – has the power to realize the potential of an intimate relationship, while the suspicion and manipulativeness suggested by the above saying promises its destruction.

Directing this stance at one's children is no less tragic. When a parent says: "I'm not speaking to you" s/he does not only invite inauthentic placating; s/he also teaches the child that this is an acceptable response. Healthy infants do not have a need to be courted, but once children learn this pattern of behavior, they are apt to reject a hug when it is most needed. Both the older and the younger generation can play this destructive game: troubled adolescents often feel that their parents do not care, that they are not wanted and accepted by the significant adults around them. The parents, however, deny this vehemently; they love their children very much ("Look at all that we're doing for them!"), but are afraid to be exploited by them. The gap between meaning and saying is the source of often irreversible damage to the younger generation's self-esteem, resulting in further deterioration of the relationship.

What Will the Neighbors Say?

Socialization, or the process through which new members acquire the norms and customs of the group they join, is absolutely necessary for that group's smooth functioning. Parents are the major socializing agents; they are expected to impart to their children the skills necessary to become well functioning members of the society to which they belong. Good manners, etiquette, observing protocol – they all have their place in social life. But, as we have pointed out above, it is important to draw a distinction between what is allowed, perhaps even encouraged in the privacy of one's home and what is considered as appropriate behavior in public. An insistence on decorum, underlying such sayings as "Don't wash your dirty laundry in public" or "What will they think of us?", conveys the additional message that it is important to appear better than we actually are, that appearances are better than reality. We (our children, our marriage, our relatives; also our group or entire culture) do not stand up to the observer's criteria, so we have to pretend. The outside observer has become more consequential than the self. There is an analogy here to make-up, intended to cover imperfections, to make them temporarily invisible.

A parent may order a child: "Keep your voice down! No need for the entire neighborhood to hear you!" At Layer C the message is that the need to express one's pain is less important than placating one's parents, who, in turn, want to placate their social environment. This is one of the roots of the pseudo-self (Bowen, 1976a): children learn to hide their feelings. Instead of attending to their own authentic needs, they invest energy in the needs and demands of others. As the self becomes of marginal value, anxiety increases and obstructs insight. In some cultures this process may be more pronounced for girls than for boys; the former are taught not to hearken to their own needs (sex, aggression, curiosity), but rather to fulfill those of others.

Warning someone about "what will the neighbors say" carries an additional message: "Don't be selfish, be considerate of others." Indeed, it is very important to be aware of the needs of those around us (do not practice your drum solo at 2 a.m.). Yet being attentive to one's own wants and needs has crucial significance, as well. The underlying message of the above saying creates individuals who are unaware of what they want, tend to be anxious about their appearance, and in extreme cases may cover up physical abuse. Their overly high need for the positive opinion of others results in dependence, indecisiveness, conformity, obedience. Concern for the neighbors' opinion is also central to pseudo-mutual families, where there is little closeness and intimacy, but there are many ceremonial acts (such as birthday parties, anniversaries, etc), for others to see. Individuals in such families are lonely; their needs are neither expressed nor met, for "the show must go on." Ask them, how they are, and they may be unable to answer beyond the routine "fine, thank you," never having been truly asked. Just think of the child who is perfunctorily asked every day: "How was it at school?", and who then answers, in the same vein: "It was OK." In this painful dynamics, the more you hurt, the less you are able to share. You must appear strong, able, coping. Rigidity results, combined with anger and envy aimed at those who are authentic.

In Chapter 3 we introduced the question of a multicultural perspective. The issue we are addressing now can serve as a good example of the therapeutic dilemma raised by such a perspective, for the acceptance and even encouragement of this type of inauthenticity may be more prevalent in some cultures than in others (e.g. in collectivistic rather than individualistic ones). Introducing some clients to authenticity may create for them crises and dangers.

Forgive and Forget!

This saying overlaps with "let bygones be bygones," "turn over a new leaf," or "let's move on": in all of these something unpleasant has happened – so unpleasant that it has to be buried. The source appears to be magnanimous, willing to both *forgive* the other's transgression and to *forget* it. While forgiving is certainly preferable to holding a grudge (see Chapter 9, below), it necessarily reinforces an already existing power differential between forgiver and the one forgiven. (For some further aspects of apologizing and forgiving see Kramer-Moore and Moore, 2002, pp. 167–168; 2003). Whatever the sin was, it has been forgiven, and perhaps even forgotten (though see below), but several new agendas are now created, such as:

1. I expect some gratitude.
2. Should the tables be turned, I expect you to forgive me.
3. I forgive you now, but watch out in the future!

The last of these is especially problematic, for it assumes some responsibility on the part of the "sinner," who is expected not to relapse. How this is to be achieved is unclear, particularly when there is no discussion of the underlying issues. Has there been any change in either of the participants to believe that the same behavior will not be repeated? The boozer, the abuser, the shoplifter, the liar – what reason is there for them to adopt a different mode of relating to their environment?

   As for forgetting – since it is not known to occur on command, this suggestion to intentionally hide something from ourselves must, by necessity, involve some deception. "We'll both pretend this thing hasn't happened." The short-term gains of such a cover-up are offset by its long-term losses. Some temporary quiet has been arranged, but the cause of the falling-out has not been dealt with. "Putting all of this behind us" assumes that conflicts can be artificially terminated. Yet in families nothing is ever forgotten. Whenever tension rises, the old list is opened; Guerin and Guerin (1976, p. 98) referred to this as the family's "bitter bank."

Activities

1 A word to the wise

See Activity number 1 in Chapter 5.

2 Hidden Agenda 1

This activity can be used to introduce authentic and congruent communication.

Trigger: Give each family member slips of paper. Write on each slip of paper the name of a family member, and something you think but are not ready to say to that person. Don't reveal what you write.

Possible points for discussion:

How to say what we think, without it becoming a weapon?
How to say what we think, so that the listener can benefit, rather than lose?

3 Hidden Agenda 2

At the following meeting repeat the previous activity with a change.
   Trigger: Write on each slip of paper the name of a family member, and something you think s/he feels toward you but hasn't dared to mention. Don't reveal what you write.

Possible points for discussion:

Whom are we defending when we do not reveal our feelings: Is it the other person or is it us?
What do we gain, and what do we lose by not saying what we feel?
How can we give feedback without hurting the listener?

4 Objects

Trigger: At the preceding meeting ask each family member to bring to this session a meaningful object, one that signifies something typical or important about this family (e.g. a trophy, a book, a plate, a snapshot) without discussing their choice with the others. Now each person, in his or her turn, places the chosen object in the centre, without explaining. The rest share their thoughts about what each object (chosen by another) means for them, what are their associations, why it was chosen, in their opinion. When all are done, the therapist prompts them to add anything else that has not been mentioned this far.
   Now ask each "owner" to tell whether s/he has been understood in this choice, or were the others projecting their own stories into the object.

What object haven't you brought?
Have you learned anything new about the family?
Have you learned anything new about yourself?

5 *Dinner time*

Trigger: This is a guided imagination activity. Darken the room, speak slowly, in a relaxed, low voice: Sit in a comfortable position, close your eyes, breathe deeply.

Think of a recent family dinner. Try to remember every person who sat around the table. Try to recall the conversation that took place. [pause] Breathe deeply, move your limbs, open your eyes slowly. Turn on the lights.

Possible points for discussion:

How did you feel about yourself during this dinner?
Who did most of the talking?
Who was quiet most of the time?
How would you describe each person's feelings and thoughts during this meal?
Give each of them a sentence that you think expresses them but they didn't say it [e.g. "I wish this was over..."; "Why can't we have such a nice dinner every evening?"; "What I would most like to do is . . ."]

Encourage family members to react to each other's description, without defending themselves.

6 *Packages*

Trigger: Give each family member a page with drawings of packages of different sizes, shapes, wrappings. Each is asked to assign the name of a family member, including self, to a package. For each person, think of something s/he would have in the package.

Possible points for discussion:

What do you think of the package given to you by others?
What's in your package – is it a gift or a burden?
How do these packages reflect inequality in the family?
How much of your package are you responsible for, and how much is given to you by others in the family?
Share with the rest of the family what you have learned about yourself and about others today.

7

Inequality, or What Can You Expect From a Man?

Women pinched the best part at the outset. You bet your sweet life they're not giving it up now that they've learned to play it to perfection . . . Besides, they've achieved what they've always been after: man's collective bad conscience, which gives them unbelievable advantages without their having to lift a finger. (Bergman, 1983, p. 71)

Unequal treatment of selected classes of individuals has been the rule in human societies for millennia. The basis for discrimination can be practically anything, though race, color, gender, religion, and national origin have certainly been the most frequent ones. Large-scale, official endorsement of

Destructive Myths in Family Therapy: How to Overcome Barriers to Communication by Seeing and Saying – A Humanistic Perspective, First Edition. Daniela Kramer-Moore and Michael Moore.
© 2012 John Wiley & Sons, Ltd. Published 2012 by John Wiley & Sons, Ltd.

social equality is a definite newcomer to the conduct of human affairs; its significant milestones are the United States Declaration of Independence in 1776, the 1789 Declaration of Rights during the French Revolution, and the 1948 Universal Declaration of Human Rights by the United Nations (see Box 7.1). Important as these declarations are, their implementation in everyday life has not yet been achieved in any society, let alone, universally. The Nuremberg race laws of 1935 deprived German Jews of their rights of citizenship; parts of the United States of America have treated African-Americans as second class citizens in our lifetime; Switzerland did not give its female citizens the right to vote until 1971; and not so long ago the 16-million strong Southern Baptist Convention adopted an amendment to the effect that "A wife is to submit graciously to the servant leadership of her husband" (*Time*, 1998, p. 15). The rights of women and children are trampled upon in large parts of Africa and Asia, and in some regions of India and China female infants are customarily aborted or murdered (see Arnold, Kishor, and Roy, 2002, and Hesketh, Lu, and Xing, 2005). Though many societies are changing from being driven by feudal values to being based on egalitarian principles, the typical Western family still lags behind the above quoted declarations of equality: it pays lip service to egalitarian and democratic principles, without internalizing them. These principles confuse the holders of traditional roles, require some to relinquish power, others to receive it. Democracy and its concomitant practice of equality are touted to families who often lack the maturity to fully accept them. (The inescapable connection between democracy and equality, along with justice and liberty, was established in the fourth century BCE; see Aristotle, 1946, vi (2), 1317b.) Yet if we subscribe to Article 1 of the Declaration of Human Rights, quoted below (see Box 7.1), can we in good conscience stop practicing equality in our own home? Does democracy abruptly stop at the front door?

Box 7.1   From the Universal Declaration of Human Rights

The first four articles of the Universal Declaration of Human Rights, adopted and proclaimed by the General Assembly of the United Nations on December 10, 1948 (United Nations, 1950, p. 535).

(*continued*)

Article 1: All human beings are born free and equal in dignity and rights. They are endowed with reason and conscience and should act towards one another in a spirit of brotherhood.

Article 2: Everyone is entitled to all the rights and freedoms set forth in this Declaration, without distinction of any kind, such as race, colour, sex, language, religion, political or other opinion, national or social origin, property, birth or other status. Furthermore, no distinction shall be made on the basis of the political, jurisdictional or international status of the country or territory to which a person belongs, whether it be independent, trust, non-self-governing or under any other limitation of sovereignty.

Article 3: Everyone has the right to life, liberty and security of person.

Article 4: No one shall be held in slavery or servitude; slavery and the slave trade shall be prohibited in all their forms.

An important lesson about the costs and benefits of democracy in small-groups can be learned from a series of field experiments conducted by Kurt Lewin and his colleagues (e.g. Lewin, Lippitt, and White, 1939). In these classical, ground-breaking studies the authors imposed democratic vs. autocratic leaders on groups of boys engaged in simple tasks, such as mask making or model construction. Groups working in an autocratic atmosphere had slightly higher productivity than their democratically led counterparts, while the latter produced higher quality, more creative items. Members of democratic groups were more spontaneous, fact-minded and friendly, relating to their leader on an "equality basis." In contrast, the groups of autocratic leaders showed more hostility and aggressive domination to each other, became apathetic, and behaved submissively toward their leader.

The Status of Children

An application of these findings (and of much of their subsequent confirmation) to families raises the sticky issue of so called "parental authority." To what extent do we want children (not to mention wives) to blindly obey family authority figures, and to what lengths are we willing to go to ensure their obedience? As we will see in Chapter 9 (see also McCord, 1996), punishment is an ineffective method for the achievement of desired goals, and yet domestic corporal punishment of children has been abolished to date only in 29 countries, among them Germany, Greece, Israel, Sweden, and Tunisia, but not France, Japan, the United Kingdom or the United States. Physical co-ercing of children does not stop at home; corporal punishment of children in schools, acting *in loco parentis*, is legal in many countries, including 20 of the states of the United States. The undesirable effects of the corporal punish-ment of children have frequently been described by educators and psychol-ogists; Straus (1996) reviewed research evidence connecting this practice to both societal and individual violence; more recently Grogan-Kaylor (2005) found a positive correlation between corporal punishment and antisocial behavior. (Judicial corporal punishment, such as the caning of adults, is also practiced in several Asian, African and Middle Eastern countries.)

So what can parents (and teachers) do in order to help children become stable, functional adults? Baumrind's (1991) analysis provides us with a useful working model. Basing her work on previous findings that identify demandingness and responsiveness as the two major dimensions of parental behavior, she derived a fourfold classification of parenting: those who are both demanding and responsive are *authoritative* parents (often referred to as *Assertive Democratic*) – understanding and supportive, rather than in-trusive or restrictive. *Authoritarian* (strict and punitive) parents are high on demandingness and low on responsiveness, expecting obedience without explanation. Parents who are more responsive than demanding are *permis-sive* (aka *indulgent*): they are lenient and tend to avoid any confrontation with their children. Finally, those who are neither demanding nor respon-sive, have a *rejecting-neglecting* style (also known as *disengaged*; see p. 25); they neither monitor nor support their children, and can actively reject them. Empirical research has consistently associated these parenting styles with various outcomes, including academic achievement, psychopathology, and behavior problems. Thus Schaffer, Clark, and Jeglic (2008) found that maternal permissiveness contributed to students' antisocial behavior; Gunty and Buri (2008) reported that while paternal authoritarianism (i.e. the strict and punitive style) was positively related to the development of maladaptive schemas of college students, authoritativeness (i.e. the democratic-assertive style) showed an inverse relationship. In a study by Turner, Chandler, and Heffer (2009) authoritative parenting significantly predicted academic per-formance (additional research was reviewed by Maccoby, 2007). No less im-portant are the findings of Pratt et al. (1992): Authoritative vs. authoritarian parenting style correlated with the characteristics of mothers' speech toward toddlers: authoritarian mothers were more directive, less responsive, used shorter sentences, and thus were "less likely to use conversation-eliciting language styles." These authors also found that more satisfied couples spoke in longer sentences, using more complex verb phrases. They hypothesized that "the quality of the couple's relationship helps to shape a family climate, which is in turn expressed in parent-child conversations."

The picture that emerges from these (and many similar) findings is one of democratically run families raising better adjusted children. Maccoby (2007, pp. 36–37) recently summarized the literature by saying that "[T]he question underlying much modern parenting research, then, is not *whether* parents should exercise authority and children should comply but, rather, *how* parental control can best be exercised so as to support children's growing competence and self-management. Thus it is increasingly understood that strong parental agency and strong child agency are not incompatible. Both can be maintained within a system of mutually understood realms of legitimate authority, though this understanding must be progressively renegotiated as children grow older."

Since there are inevitable differences between parents and their children with respect to such crucial issues as knowledge, responsibility, earning power and so forth, there can be no perfect equality between them. Yet this need not prevent any parent from treating their children justly, respecting their rights, being attentive to their needs, and relating to them age-appropriately. In the absence of democratic principles these commendable attitudes and behaviors are likely to be replaced by lamentable ones, ranging from harsh, unjust punishment, through excessive indulgence to criminal neglect. (For cultural differences in child rearing practices see Chao, 1994, as well as Gonzalez-Mena, 2008, p. 128.)

Spousal Equality

Some of the most serious PFPs derive from family members' tendency to relate to significant others as objects. Spouses may function according to egalitarian norms in such external areas as professional expectations, economic decisions, and so on. Yet some of them have severe difficulties in accepting themselves and each other as of equal ability to bring up their children, to need and enjoy sex, to have social sensitivity, to be both emotional and rational. In spite of sharing money earning and child rearing responsibilities, some couples invest great amounts of energy in one-upmanship, in dealing with their anxiety of being undervalued and exploited; their relationship is based on the spirit of contest rather than teamwork. We have already referred to the advantages of parallel, as opposed to either complementary or symmetrical relationships (see pp. 29–30) – we now reiterate the importance of equality in spousal ties.

It is particularly helpful to look at spousal relationships through the lens of transactional analysis (TA) (Berne, 1968, 1980; Stewart and Joines, 1987). The model offered by TA identifies interpersonal communications as originating in and addressed to one of three ego-states: parent, adult, or child. In their turn, the persons addressed respond, again, from and to one of these states. In the parent ego-state one's behaviors, thoughts and feelings are indiscriminately copied from those of parent figures. Adult ego-states consist of responses appropriate to the here-and-now. Child ego-states tend to resemble reactions from one's childhood. Transactions between spouses can occur between any two of these states. Most often we would expect adult-to-adult behaviors, but many other combinations are also likely to occur: today he wants to be babied by her, and tomorrow they reverse these roles; they may both act like parents, gravely discussing the future of their children (or the children of the neighbors); occasionally they may even delight in consentaneous childish behavior. Inequality appears on the scene when there is a consistent pattern of one spouse "talking down" to the other (parent-to-child ego states). This is the position taken by the sources of the following sayings.

It's for your own good!

A dramatic and compelling argument against the use of this message in child rearing has been made by Alice Miller. Miller has written extensively on the subject of what has been called *poisonous pedagogy*, that is, traditional child rearing methods that are aimed at breaking children's will at an early age. A few examples appear in Box 7.2.

Box 7.2   Spare the rod and spoil the child?

Our first two examples were collected by Katharina Rutschky, a German educator, to illustrate *poisonous pedagogy*; they appear in Miller (1990). The mid-eighteenth century German texts on child-rearing from which these excerpts are taken may not have had a wide circulation, yet they are representative of traditional methods of education:

(*continued*)

1. "I advise all those whose concern is the education of children to make it their main occupation to drive out wilfulness and wickedness and to persist until they have reached their goal. As I have remarked above, it is impossible to reason with young children . . . If parents are fortunate enough to drive out wilfulness from the very beginning by means of scolding and the rod, they will have obedient, docile, and good children . . . ."

2. "If your son does not want to learn because it is your will, if he cries with the intent of defying you, if he does harm in order to offend you, in short, if he insist on having his own way: *Then whip him well till he cries so: Oh no, Papa, oh no!* Such disobedience amounts to a declaration of war against you. Your son is trying to usurp your authority, and you are justified in answering force with force in order to ensure his respect . . . ."

These 250-year-old methods are a thing of the past, are they not? But look at just two examples of what any one of the millions of Internet surfers may find if they search for advice on child-rearing. These vignettes come from *Focus on the Family* (2005):

Spanking typically works best with ages 2 to 6. It should be used only for specific, purposeful misbehavior and should never be done in anger. As with other techniques, spanking should be used as one of many discipline tools.

You've heard the reprimand "Hold your tongue!" Make your child do it — literally. Have her stick out her tongue and hold it between two fingers. This is an especially effective correction for public outbursts.

How do babies come into the world? The best way for a baby to come into the world is through the love of a married man and woman. Sadly, this doesn't happen all the time. However, God's best plan is for a baby to be born with a mother and father that are married. Marriage is God's best idea to create a family for years to come.

According to *Physician* magazine, spanking should be used selectively for clear, deliberate misbehavior, especially a child's persistent defiance

(continued)

of a parent. It should be used only when the child receives at least as much praise for good behavior as correction for problem behavior. Verbal correction, time out and logical consequences should be used initially, followed by spanking when noncompliance persists . . . . Spanking is inappropriate before 15 months of age, should be less necessary after 6 years, and rarely, if ever, used after 10 years of age. Spanking should always be administered in private. Appropriate spanking only leaves temporary redness of skin, and never bruises or injures. Spanking works, but must be used thoughtfully and carefully in conjunction with other disciplinary measures. (These Last Days Ministries, 2010)

In her book, appropriately titled *For Your Own Good,* Miller (1990) found that "The conviction that parents are always right and that every act of cruelty, whether conscious or unconscious, is an expression of their love is . . . deeply rooted in human beings" (p. 5). Here are some of the motives attributed by Miller (1987, pp. 97–98) to poisonous parents:

1. the unconscious need to pass on to others the humiliation one has undergone;
2. the need to possess and have at one's disposal an object to manipulate;
3. the need to idealize one's childhood and one's parents;
4. fear of freedom;
5. fear of the reappearance of what one has repressed; and
6. revenge for the pain one has suffered.

While the *It's for your own good!* message is most commonly sent by parents to their children, it is easy to imagine situations where it is used towards a spouse or a friend. It can appear in trivial situations: how to dress, what to eat, which book to read. But it is also used in more important, sometimes highly significant settings: what to study, whom to marry, where to live, what ideology to endorse. *It's for your own good!* belittles the other, lets its source gain points at the other's expense: "You don't know enough, I'm better, wiser, more experienced than you are." It reveals a complete lack of empathy, with the unsolicited advice coming from the source's preconceptions, not from the other's point of view or needs. The core of the message is one's need to control others, to make sure they walk in the source's path. On further examination we are likely to find that the recommended behavior is for the source's own good, reinforcing his/her perception of "what is right," showing off as a caring person, who is involved in the other's life.

Honor your father

"Show me some respect!" is often said or implied by parents, teachers and other authority figures. The demand for veneration bases itself on formidable sources, for it appears in the scriptures of all major religions and religious philosophies. In the Hebrew Bible it is the fifth of the Ten Commandments, and comes with a promise (and an inferred threat): "Honor your father and your mother, so that you may live long in the land the Lord your God is giving you." It is repeated in the New Testament, where, by no mere coincidence, it is followed by "Slaves, obey your earthly masters with respect and fear." It appears in the Koran as the second most important commitment of Muslims, in Hinduism as one of the Laws of Manu, and has an entire Confucian book devoted to it. But let us stop and reflect for a moment: What does it exactly mean to *demand* respect? After all, to hold someone in high esteem is the natural, well-deserved outcome of his or her behavior. Unless, of course, two conditions obtain: the source demanding respect is both unworthy and powerful. Then authenticity and congruence are sacrificed in the interest of physical or emotional survival: regardless of what they do, mighty authorities must be respected (or else).

Parents' demand for respect is always a response to what they consider to be a lack of respect. Instead of looking for the source of the problem (probably themselves), they try to regain control by insisting on an empty gesture, similar in its dynamics to "Say you're sorry!", "Apologize!", or "You should be grateful!" (cf. Morman and Floyd, 2006, p. 51. For more on the psychology of apologizing, see Kramer-Moore and Moore, 2003). All of these are expressions of a need for control, for domination. They teach a dysfunctional behavior pattern of appeasing and groveling.

Here are some Layer B messages conveyed by this saying.

1. I enjoy forcing you to comply.
2. I don't care what you really think and feel, all I want is to hear some words that will make me feel better.
3. Let's not stop and reflect on why you don't respect me.
4. I believe in "word magic" or the mistaking of words for deeds (see Moore, 1999).

5. Our age and/or power difference is in itself a sufficient reason for giving me respect.
6. I subscribe to Machiavelli's advice to princes (repeated by the Red Queen in the recent movie version of *Alice in Wonderland*): "it is far safer to be feared than loved."

We shall not discuss here the possible merits of Machiavelli's advice; suffice it to say that the principles on which healthy families and other intimate relationship are run differ from those that may be useful for the management of large organizations. While it is quite possible that manipulations, secretiveness, the encouragement of rivalry, and even the use of spying and deception are vital to some large-scale operations, they are toxic as far as parenthood, spousehood or friendship is concerned.

I'm glad we had this little talk

Here is an overheard conversation between a student and a teacher at the high school library. The teacher lectured her student for about 20 minutes: what he should and should not have done. Why he has failed, and how he has disappointed. She asked him once: "Do you understand what I'm saying?" and he replied: "Yes, ma'm." When she finally ran out of steam, she said: "You can go back to class now. I'm glad we had this talk." Some parents are also in the habit of holding monologues with their children, being unaware of both their futility and the damage they cause. Instead of bringing about understanding and closeness, they promote selective (in)attention, where the listener's only motivation is for the painful encounter to be over. No wonder, such talks often end in "How many times have I told you . . . ."

A generation gap is not necessary for these ineffective episodes; they can take place in sibling and spousal relationships, as well. In the latter case, the course of the interaction is likely to depend on the type of non-egalitarian relationship the spouses have (see Chapter 2): In a complementary bond one preaches, while the other clams up; in a symmetrical one they try to out-shout each other. In none of these cases is there a genuine attempt to relate to the other person at eye level, to encourage feedback, to share feelings, and to listen. These teachers, parents and spouses look down at their partners, emphasizing and (perhaps unconsciously) enjoying – at the expense of conducting functional communication – their real or imagined power differential. What they all lack is the willingness to participate in a dialogue.

In a description of two very different styles of discourse Matson (1986, p. 157), wrote that monologues belong to totalitarian systems; their purpose is to *command* rather than to *commune*; they are concerned with persuasion rather than participation. Dialogues are authentic communication; they imply tolerance of ambiguity, they open possibilities for discussion and dissent. "In dialogue," wrote Foley (2003), "people learn how to come together to understand the thought processes of others . . . . The culture that is promoted in the dialogues is one of respect, with the goal of trying to understand, not to argue against others' views" (pp. 248, 250; see also Taylor, 1991, p. 33 on the fundamentality of the dialogue). Unless we parents, spouses, teachers or friends can internalize these basic principles of the dialogue, there is little chance for our "little talks" to have any effect other than frustration and alienation.

It's not the same thing

"I can't go on with this marriage," says the desperate daughter to her mother, hoping for some understanding. "But you married him for better or worse!" says the mother (who does not want a divorced daughter and two grandchildren moving in with her). "But you divorced Dad, didn't you?" says the daughter, looking for some consistency in her confused circumstances. "It's not the same thing!" responds her mom.

A similar thought process can be found in many other situations.

- My mother can't help because she is busy, tired, or sick; yours is just uncooperative.
- I yell at the children when they deserve it; you always lose your temper.
- I have my reasons for what I've done; you are just thoughtless.

Then there are these well-known semantic games, again based on making fine distinctions when they serve our purposes:

- You're stingy; I economize.
- I'm cautious; you're a coward.
- You're obese; I'm overweight.
- I'm thorough; you're pedantic.

Of course, in a strictly formal sense all of these statements are true: If no two snowflakes are identical, then certainly no two human situations can ever be exactly the same. (See Moore, 2001, for a discussion of the continuum ranging from "everything is the same" to "everything is different.") But we doubt that any of these individuals are influenced by such logical considerations. Instead, they are all likely to be subject to the human weakness so well described by the biblical mote and beam conceit: They are blind to the very same defects in themselves which they are quick to point out in others.

A word of warning: Sometimes a cigar is a cigar. It is possible that one partner is domineering/stingy/unstable while the other is not. As with other sayings, one has to differentiate between myth and reality.

I told you so

Whenever this is said, the source implies: "I know better, and now I've proved it!" Something surprising has happened. If it is a pleasant surprise ("I told you you'd pass the test! You needn't have worried. I told you you'd be OK!") – there is less of a problem, though there is a power differential even in this situation. If the outcome is an unpleasant one, where the target has been hurt, his/her self-esteem has been lowered, saying "I told you so" is equivalent to kicking someone who is already down. "You're so stupid! I saw this coming, but you wouldn't listen!" The target's weakness is exploited in order to build up the source's ego. The source may add: "Let this be a lesson to you!" – that is to say: "I hope that in the future you'll listen to me and not to yourself." Of course, "objectively" speaking, the source may be right, and his or her original advice may have been correct. There are, however, two fundamental problems with this claim.

1. The objective or factual state of affairs has only secondary importance in interpersonal relations, where one's perception of oneself and of the other determine both the process and the outcome of an encounter. "The only reality you can possibly know is the world as *you* perceive and experience it at this moment," wrote Rogers (1990d, p. 424) in his discussion of the phenomenological nature of all human life. This is not a vague, philosophical statement of no practical consequence. Rather, it alerts us to the possibility or even the likelihood that our collocutors live in worlds different from ours, that they interpret our words and gestures differently from what we intended and that we may misinterpret their reactions to our behavior. By giving priority to our perception of the world we take a controlling and disparaging view of incidents experienced by others, we undervalue their frame of reference and we empower ourselves at their expense. Even if the bottom

line proves us right, the costs of belittling others by diminishing their feelings of self-worth, and the damage to our relationship can be great.

2. Giving advice, especially when it is unsolicited, invites a sense of failure for at least one of the two participants: for the advisor, when the advice is either ignored, rejected, or turns out to have been wrong, and for the advisee, who lost a chance to solve a problem independently, has been misled, or feels bad for having refused to listen. Instead of energizing, *I told you so* paralyzes, makes the target lose self-confidence: s/he might freeze, both in order not to fail again and not to prove the source right.

Activities

1 A word to the wise

See Activity number 1 in Chapter 5.

2 Line up

Trigger: Create a long line across the room (drawing it on the floor by chalk, arranging chairs in a row etc.), and label by a sign one end as "Very Important", and the other as "Not Important At All". (You may wish to use other labels, more appropriate for this family, such as Privileged to Disadvantaged, Respected to Disrespected and so on.) Ask family members to place themselves along the line, according to their perceived position in the family.

Possible points for discussion:

Reflect on the process of choosing where to stand.
What are your feelings when in that position?
If you could change your place, where would you stand?
What needs to happen for such change to occur?
What is the relationship between your position in the family and in the outside world?

3 A piece of cake

Trigger: Give each family member a page with five circles drawn on it. These are pies of love, attention, respect, blame, responsibility, control, dominance, worth – choose the ones you think are most relevant to this family.

Once the labels are decided cut up each pie, giving each person the slice they actually have in the family. Add a red flag to the pieces you consider too big or too small.

Possible points for discussion:

Look at the different perceptions of family members and try to empathize
   with them.
What are the gains and losses of having unequal pieces for individuals and
   for the family as a unit?
What changes would you like to see in the sizes of the pieces?

4 Favoritism

Trigger: Think about your family of origin: who felt unequal there? Who thought that there was some favoritism in the family?

Possible points for discussion:

What caused this feeling, and what did it do to that person?
There were probably some family members who tried to convince this
   person that s/he was wrong, that all received equal treatment. Did s/he
   believe this?
Think of your current family: Can you identify a similar pattern?
What can you do to prevent the same thing happening?

5 Respect me!

Trigger: Think of an incident where someone demanded that you show him/her more respect. What were the underlying dynamics of this event? [pause] Now recall an incident where it was you who felt that you deserved more respect than you received from someone.

Points for discussion:

What are the results of *demanding* respect?
What are the short- and long-term costs and gains of such a demand?
What has to change in these dynamics for respect to be the natural outcome
   of the relationship and not something to be enforced?

6 Same or different?

Trigger: Think of a situation where someone said: "It's not the same thing." Act out this event. When done, change chairs and roles, and re-enact the event.

Points for discussion:

What were the feelings and motives of each of you in the two different roles you played?

Is it really "not the same thing"?

What do you gain and what do you lose by saying this?

What else can you say so as to be both authentic and empathic?

8

Belittling, or Who Do You Think You Are?

When Mallory had paid the check, he asked her if she wanted a cab. 'What a stupid idea,' she said, frowning with disgust, as if he had suggested squandering their savings account or putting their children on the stage. (Cheever, 1982)

Humans face a constant challenge: we must accommodate ourselves to the demands of our groups without being totally assimilated in them. Serious

Destructive Myths in Family Therapy: How to Overcome Barriers to Communication by Seeing and Saying – A Humanistic Perspective, First Edition. Daniela Kramer-Moore and Michael Moore.
© 2012 John Wiley & Sons, Ltd. Published 2012 by John Wiley & Sons, Ltd.

deviations from this compromise have dire consequences. At one extreme we risk being ostracized for being too unique even in cultures that appreciate and promote individualism; at the other, the total loss of individuality maybe criticized even in collectivist societies. To negotiate these dialectics individuals need a sense of worth, a considerable degree of respect for themselves; in short, they must possess some self-esteem. The importance of this personality concept is far reaching: self-esteem is the sine qua non of mental health, of the fulfillment of one's potential, of the ability to adapt to changing situations. It serves as the basis for the successful maintenance of mature intimate relationships, as well as for the esteem of others: Those who dislike themselves find it very difficult to like anyone else. One of Maslow's deficiency needs (1970), self-esteem is valued by those who have it and is being sought by those who lack it. It is a product of early experiences, greatly influenced by the feedback one receives from significant others during childhood. Satir (1988, pp. 20–21) coined a useful metaphor by referring to self-esteem or self-worth as a "pot": One's pot may be full of energy and positive thoughts, or may be lacking in these, or it may contain distress, anger, frustration and feelings of worthlessness. Satir attached great importance to self-esteem: "I am convinced that the crucial factor in what happens both *inside* people and *between* people is one's self-worth, one's pot" (p. 22).

A significant source for the shaping of one's self-esteem can be found in comparing oneself to others; the pervasive phenomenon of social comparison (Suls, Martin, and Wheeler, 2002) provides one with a perception of relative standing. Evaluating oneself through finding faults in others offers a foolproof method for gaining some sense of self-esteem: just find someone who is worth less than you, and if you cannot find one, create one! This is the mechanism behind belittling: gaining illusory ascendance by disparaging others, saying or implying that they are unimportant, ineffective or unsuccessful. Two brief cases of belittling appear in Box 8.1.

Box 8.1 Two illustrations of belittling

Though a specific act of belittling may be over in a few seconds, a style of belittling in a relationship may endure for decades:

- A couple in their eighties have a long history of belittling. For much of their married life the successful university professor looked

(continued)

down not only on his less well-educated wife, but also on her friends and their families, never failing to belittle their mundane topics of conversation. Her habitual reaction was pained silence. His health deteriorated after his retirement, enabling her to settle scores by frequent reference to his frailty. This has not stopped him from continuing to aim sarcastic remarks at her.

- For as long as their marriage lasted, this professional man's wife used every opportunity to belittle both his character and his activities: His family of origin was less respectable than hers, his outlook on life was impractical, he lacked child-rearing skills, he could have earned more by a wiser career choice. In therapy sessions her behavior was found to be a reaction to her low self-esteem; this, in turn, was related to her mother's habitual belittling of her intellectual capabilities. The marriage ended in divorce.

Types of Belittling

Costly and dysfunctional as it may be, belittling is a coping mechanism: it provides immediate (though often short-lived) relief from a feeling of worthlessness. It constitutes a type of emotional abuse; psychoanalytical interpreters have found its roots in fear of engulfment and of abandonment (e.g. Green, 1998). Belittling can operate directly, by straightforwardly deprecating another's traits, achievements, looks, and so forth. Regardless of the exact words, the message is always the same: "You're not good enough!"; "You should have/could have done better!" The belittler also conveys a covert (Layer B) message: "I am better than you; I am in a position to pass judgment on you!" Belittling is also an essential element in all acts of bullying and other types of aggression; through being submitted to verbal, emotional, physical or sexual abuse, the victims of belittling are shown to be weaker than their opponent. Sarcasm, mocking, joking at the other's expense are oblique types of belittling; here a protesting victim may suffer the further indignity of "not being able to take a joke." Stereotypical belittling is also indirect, leaving its targets unable to defend themselves: "I didn't say anything about you, personally. All I said was that men are pigs/women are too emotional/academics are detached from reality!"

Another possibility is belittling oneself. Those who are constantly clown-ing, goofing off and playing the fool, are trying to preempt others from belittling them. While those who belittle others tend to be *blamers*, the behavior of self-belittlers bears some similarity to the dysfunctional com-munication pattern of the *placator* (see p. 74): Their low self-esteem leads them to appease others by providing some slapstick entertainment.

Targets and Consequences

The targets of belittling must, by necessity, be vulnerable in some respect. Relatively worthless as one may feel, it would not be a good survival tech-nique to insult those who have the authority or the physical resources to harm one. The most obvious group that fulfils these criteria, and one that is readily available within families, is children. Typically, parents employ this strategy more often to one child than to the others, thus selecting a scape-goat onto whom they can channel their frustrations. Comparisons are often involved (see "Why can't you be like your sister?" in Chapter 10), leading to further possible repercussions, such as unhealthy coalition formations, triangulations, and rivalry. In another painful form of belittling parents push a child to outstanding achievements in sports, arts, or academic en-deavors, thereby signaling that: (a) they are not good enough, since they are not performing to their best ability; and (b) their acceptance by their parent is conditional. We must mention, in passing, that in their *in loco parentis* status, teachers occasionally employ the very same tactics toward some of their wards, disparaging them when they fail, comparing them to one another or to their older siblings, pushing them aggressively and at a high future cost toward higher and higher achievements.

Belittling children is a particularly insidious act, for it has two dysfunc-tional consequences. The first is based on the concept of the "looking-glass self," proposed over a century ago. The sociologist Charles Cooley (1902) attributed the development of the self to the perceptions of our behaviors by others (see also mirroring in Kohut, 1971, p. 116). Thus children learn about themselves by observing how others, and especially their parents, react to them. If they are belittled, they are likely to internalize the negative evaluations they receive and to develop a negative self-image (Cook and Douglas, 1998). Indirect empirical evidence for this is found in research on bullying, also known as peer abuse (see Box 8.2). Hawker and Boulton's (2000) review found a clear association between peer victimization and psychosocial maladjustment, especially depression. Juhnke, Granello, and

Granello (2011) reviewed research connecting bullying with suicidal behavior. In a large UK survey Wolke and Skew (2011) found a dose-response relationship: children who were bullied both at home and at school had the strongest association with behavior problems (up to 14 times increased), and were the least happy compared to those not victimized in either context. Others have reported even more severe consequences of peer victimization. Studies by both Schreier et al. (2009) and Arsenault et al. (2011) found psychotic symptoms in 12-year-olds who had been bullied.

Box 8.2   Who bullies whom?

Prevalence

Though the exact definition of bullying may change from country to country, recent surveys of bullying at school leave no doubt about the seriousness of this problem:

- In England 47 percent report being bullied at age 14 (name calling, threat of violence, social exclusion, forced to hand over money or possessions; see Green, Collingwood, and Ross, 2010).
- A survey conducted by the Centers for Disease Control and Prevention (2011) in Massachusetts found that between a quarter and a third of 11- to 16-year-olds reported having been bullied (repeatedly teased, threatened, hit, kicked, or excluded by another student or group of students).
- A worldwide survey of school-aged children by the World Health Organization (2004) found levels of bullying (at least twice a month) ranging from 1 to 50 percent across all countries and regions and age/gender groups.

Victims

While all children are likely to experience occasional harassment by their peers, Smith, Shu, and Madsen (2001) found that the victims of bullying are those who are perceived to be weak, shy, non-assertive, disabled, or otherwise different. They add that those among the harassed who cope less well and receive less adequate social support are the targets of continued victimization.

(continued)

A longitudinal study of over 15,000 young people in England found that intact family units reduced the threat of their children being bullied. Those living in step- or single parent families, or not living with either of their biological parents were more likely to be bullied and to report threats of violence or actual violence (Green, Collingwood, and Ross, 2010). The authors of this study hypothesized that children living in such families experience instability, feel more vulnerable, lack confidence, and are more sensitive to bullying, as well as more likely to become victims. This study also found that children who had to provide care for someone disabled or sick in their household (and who were consequently socially isolated from their peers) were more likely to report being bullied.

Bullies

A literature review by Batsche and Knoff (1994; see also Baldry and Farrington, 2000) found that bullying, similarly to other parental behaviors, is often transgenerational: children bullied at home tend to react by bullying their weaker peers at school. They often come from homes where their authoritarian parents (see Chapter 7) teach them to strike back when provoked. Their high need for control, combined with a lack of empathy, endow their bullying episodes with reinforcing power, by making them feel more secure and less anxious. Glew, Rivara, and Feudtner (2000) concurred: in their study bullies were found to have a strong desire for power, they seemed to enjoy being in control, and craved social influence. Their aggressive behavior was reinforced by the prestige they gained, as well as by the material goods coerced from their victims.

Research on bullies' self-esteem provides conflicting evidence: It is unclear whether they have higher or lower self-esteem than other children. Pollastri, Cardemil, and O'Donnell (2010) suggested that we distinguish between "pure bullies" and "bully/victims," where the latter are both bullied and bullying. In their study of middle-school students in two cities in the northeast United States they found that while bully/victims had significantly lower self-esteem than either pure bullies or students not involved in bullying, the self-esteem of pure bullies did not significantly differ from that of non-involved students.

The second consequence of belittling children is the by now familiar mechanism of transgenerational transfer (see pp. 2–3, above). Having experienced belittling and suffered its first consequence, these children are now primed to do the same first to their friends and their younger siblings, then to their own spouses and children. The vicious circle of abused-abuser is at work here. As in other, analogous cases, it would be wrong to conclude that most of those who have suffered this treatment will do the same to their children, yet we can say with confidence that among those who belittle, there is a sizable proportion of such that were themselves belittled as children (cf. Glasser et al., 2001). We can again compare this conclusion with results of research on bullying: Pollastri, Cardemil, and O'Donnell (2010) found that among a sample of American firth and sixth graders, about three out of four bullies had been themselves victims of bullying.

The other potential arena for belittling is found in the spousal connection. In marriages that are not based on equality, either one spouse sits practically always in the driver's seat, or there is an on-going power struggle between the spouses (see *complementary* vs. *symmetrical* marriages, respectively, in Chapter 2). In both cases, there is fertile ground for belittling, either by the more powerful spouse, who uses this method to maintain the existing power differential, or by both spouses, with each attempting to chalk up some points. Lacking a conscious effort to change them, these behaviors tend to persist over long periods of time, because they are reinforced: there is a feeling of power in being able to make one's opponent feel small and unimportant. In family therapy we see some clients so well-versed in belittling that, when attempting not to use it, they can find no alternative way to communicate with each other.

But what is all this talk about opponents, are we not talking of marriage? Let us keep in mind that not all intact marriages are equally happy, and that couples who seek assistance from counselors, social workers, and therapists are probably a minority of those in need. It is these spouses (located at the second or third step on the continuum of blindness, mentioned in Chapter 1) who can benefit most from realizing the costs of belittling: loss of intimacy and affection. It is also worth remembering that, perhaps partially due to some disillusionment with the myth of "happily ever after" (see in Chapter 6), we are witnessing well-documented changes in the number of marriages (descending), age at first marriage (ascending), and divorce rates (around 45 percent) in much of the Western world (see, for example, ONS, 2009 and Popenoe and Whitehead, 2007).

During therapy most clients tend to identify soon enough the costs they pay in their family life for the use of belittling: at first silences, distrust, feigned indifference, stress, and fights, then lies, secrets, coalitions formed against the belittler, and a search for intimacy with a more understanding partner. All this sums up to loss of enjoyment of spousehood and family life. In spite of *seeing* all this, belittlers offer much resistance to change and when under stress, tend to regress to old patterns of behavior after some change does occur. Deeper insight into their behavior provides some hints.

- They have no alternative, so they use what they are familiar with.
- The price paid by the entire family is outweighed by the control and power gained by the belittler; giving up this control would be anxiety provoking.
- Belittlers tend to be self-centered. Giving up this stance would involve seeing the needs of others, giving them equal space; this, in turn, is painful and threatening.
- Their self-image includes a disbelief in being able to behave congruently, as well as a false sense of superiority. Learning a new pattern of behavior would put them in the lower-status position of a novice.
- A meaningful change requires a long, painful journey: looking at oneself, acknowledging one's low self-esteem, and empowering oneself through other means, instead of belittling.

The belittled also contribute to these dysfunctional dynamics:

- they may derive some secondary benefits of being the victim, pitied by other family members, belonging to a coalition of the weak;
- like many other victims, they may feel that they deserve what they get; and
- similarly to belittlers, the belittled themselves do not know how to use congruent communication or how to ask for it.

We should point out, however, that the value attributed to intimacy and affection within a close relationship such as marriage is culture dependent. Current Western conceptions about the ideal level of closeness and trust between partners (cf. analogous cultural differences in authenticity and equality, discussed in Chapters 6 and 7) are unlikely to be present in societies practicing arranged or forced marriage; there the use of belittling-type tactics may be entrenched because they serve the socially approved domination of males over females. In a similar fashion, cultures and faiths that prescribe obedience (of wife to husband, children to parents) and whose ethos includes stratification and belittling, will put little value on emotional intimacy.

Another caveat regarding intimacy and self-disclosure concerns psychopathology. For individuals suffering from various personality disorders (avoidant, paranoid, schizoid, schizotypal, and, to some extent, narcissistic; see American Psychiatric Association, 2000) intimacy and the resultant loss of total control in a relationship tend to be anxiety provoking. For them belittling is instrumental in keeping significant others at arm's length, both physically and metaphorically.

In addition to what we consider as a severe loss in the quality of the relationship, belittling one's spouse has another disagreeable result. If it is taken seriously, it implies that the belittler has married someone of lower value; this, of course, reflects poorly on the belittler. In family therapy we occasionally see a solution to this problem that serves the individual but is dysfunctional for the family. It involves a spouse who belittles his/her partner at home ("You're a failure at business", "You're childish") but praises the same to outsiders ("She is so well educated", "He is such a great cook"). A frequently observed root of this double message is the belittling spouse's (often the lesser-earning one's) need to get back at the apparently more successful partner. This ploy works for one's children, as well, when a parent puts the child down within the family circle, but is proud of it in front of strangers. The gap produced between these two messages is an example of *incongruity*, described in Chapter 6. It well illustrates the point made by Satir: "unless any family communication leads to realness or a straight, single meaning it cannot possibly lead to the trust and love necessary to nourish family members" (1988, p. 83).

Let us look also at the belittlers and find out whether their lot has improved. We have suggested that the roots of belittling are found in the attempt to raise one's low self-esteem by lowering someone else's. Research on adolescent bullying bears out this interpretation: Pollastri, Cardemil and O'Donnell (2010) reported not only relatively low self-esteem scores among bullies, but also found an increase, over time, in the self-esteem of bullying girls. Given our analogy between belittling and bullying, these findings imply that those who persistently abuse their peers (or their subordinates) have learned to cope with their low sense of self-worth by resorting to a sort of instrumental or controlled aggression (see Bushman and Anderson, 2001). So "successful" belittlers are both able to lower their partner's (or children's) self-esteem and increase their own: but how is this likely to affect their relationship? Will the belittled partner become more loving, trusting or loyal? Or will s/he lose confidence and turn more frustrated, bitter, and apt to seek solace elsewhere? Will s/he be more communicative, ready to share feelings and thoughts, or will s/he be more secretive, prone to passive-aggressive silences and to depression?

Belittling is a destructive PFP, it undermines trust, harms relationships, and destroys the ability for authentic communication or self disclosure. In this book we do not deal much with interpersonal situations that occur outside the family. Yet it is worth keeping in mind that various types of belittling can occur in other social situations, ranging from walking over co-workers or roommates, all the way to clashes between nations, cultures, and religions. Wherever it occurs, belittling operates according to the same principles as it does within the family, and has similar consequences. Belittlers try to score at the expense of others and are more than likely to end up losing their social circle's trust and affection.

At the beginning of this chapter we distinguished between direct and oblique belittling. The former are quite obvious, both in their intent and in their effect. You do not ask, "What could s/he have meant?" when told that you are a slowpoke, a no-goodnik, or such a cow. So in the sayings that follow we shall mainly focus on the latter, trying to extricate the belittling that lies behind some commonly used expressions.

You are too young to understand

No doubt, persons at different developmental stages or of different genders, cultural backgrounds and personal histories have a different understanding of various events and situations. Child vs. parent, husband vs. wife, Iranians vs. Americans might witness the same happening and interpret it according to their own agenda. Accepting the right to think, feel, understand things differently from oneself is a basis of pluralism, democracy, humanism, and general mental health. So when you say "you're too young to understand," you are expressing rigidity, inability to accept the different. You are practically shutting the other up. The child or adolescent is belittled and has no recourse, for certainly s/he cannot grow up overnight. S/he is in effect told: "For several years you're going to be a little bit stupid. I don't want to discuss these issues with you."

There is another scenario where such a message is delivered: the child has seen or heard something you would rather not have him/her experienced.

The most frequently evaded topics are sex, money, and aggression. Your embarrassment and reluctance to give a full explanation are understandable. Yet saying "you're too young" will not undo the harm done, it will only leave the child confused and frightened, with a feeling that an all-powerful parent cannot or will not help in coping. Instead of owing up to this weakness, belittling adults, unsure of themselves, turn it to their advantage by disparaging the young information seeker. Now certainly there are situations where the parent must make an unpopular decision. One does not ask a 3-year-old whether s/he agrees to be vaccinated against polio or to get an antitetanus shot. Yet it is the child's right to voice an objection, and the parent's duty is to give an answer that respects this right. Therefore, parents had better listen, permit him/her to vent thoughts and feelings, and give an age-appropriate explanation that derives from the child's own concepts and experience.

This saying bears some similarity to "Just you wait until you have children of your own," but the latter has an extra cruel twist: "I'd like to see you suffer as you make me suffer now." This is a conversation stopper, with a guilt producing component. The source is condescending, inattentive, discourages dialogue. The listener has a door slammed in the face. As with all other parental behaviors, the children will more than likely use it in adulthood. But long before that, they learn not to share their world with their parents, to avoid being rejected.

You're just like your father/mother!

Children imitate their parents. Carl Whitaker (psychiatrist and family therapist) has been quoted saying that "if we are any different from our parents, it is because we have made a conscious effort." Quite apart from genetically received similarities, many behavior patterns are learned within the family, during hundreds of repeated performances: children see their parents express love, dislike, anger and joy; they hear them greet, ask, and reply; they are around when their parents hug, kiss and fight. So yes, children are more than likely to share many traits and behaviors with their parents. Our concern here is with those situations in which one parent criticizes a child by comparing him/her to the other parent: You're sharing an unattractive trait with your mother/father. Here are some of the underlying agendas:

1. The comparison is intended to scare the child and to make him/her change a behavior. Briefly put, this is another case of control.

2. The saying is judgmental, and carries a double punch: Your other parent (whom you probably adore, or at least, identify with) is a so-and-so, and so are you.
3. There is also another, not too subtle hint: I'm better than either of you! Why isn't it me that you copy?
4. By expressing this sentiment, the source is trying to undo a perceived coalition between the child and the other parent. This ploy might back-fire though, by creating the coalition s/he is trying to prevent, that of the rejected ones.

The costs of such unfavorable comparisons are paid by all of those involved. Spontaneity, so important for maintaining an intimate relationship, is lost. In the future this child will consider how some innocent acts and man-nerisms might affect the complaining parent. The relationship between the child and the other parent, rightly or wrongly perceived by the offended parent as a coalition, is also at risk. The child has been triangulated into the marital discord, and whether s/he takes sides, or tries to stay neutral by self-blaming, will suffer the consequences.

But at least you've got nice eyes

This is a left-handed compliment, similar to "You're so well dressed today" or "I like what you're trying to do to your hair." It has many versions, in which the target is consoled for having some defect: for example, looks vs. education, brain vs. brawn. Between friends and neighbors this could well be a case of mere tactlessness. The target will be offended, and one might ask, what the motivation behind this is. But when this is said within the family, or in any other intimate relationship, it is a different matter. Chances are that it has been said more than once, and has become a "family truth."

What did the source really want to achieve?

1. Aggrandize self at the expense of the other, as in all cases of belittling?
2. Get back for something the other has done?
3. Strike out at the other out of envy?

Whatever the underlying motive (and it is likely to be a Layer C message), at the surface level it is expressed in terms of good intentions. What can the other do? If insulted, s/he is exaggerating (see "You're oversensitive," below).

If s/he puts up with it, self-esteem is lowered even more than it was prior to the conversation.

It's all your fault

The *Picture Frustration Study* developed by Saul Rosenzweig (1988) presents test-takers with a series of frustrating situations (such as being splashed by a car near the curb, date is very late for meeting, woken up by a wrong-number call, etc.), and are asked to provide a verbal response. The latter fall into three categories: blaming the source of the frustration (e.g. "You should drive more carefully!"), blaming oneself for what has happened ("I stood too close to the puddle"), or denying the frustration ("It's really nothing, just a little water"). While each of these three types of responses may be appropriate in a given situation, those who show a consistent pattern of blaming others, blaming themselves, or escaping into denial, are not coping well with their social or physical environment. Our concern here is with the first type: Satir's blamers (1988, p. 87) who always look for the guilty party when something goes wrong. "After all," they might think, "whatever has happened is bad enough, without my having to blame myself for it!"

The problem with such shrugging off of responsibility is twofold. On the one hand, it prevents effective coping with the problem that lies behind this situation, on the other hand, it is apt to make the blamed person feel belittled, bad, guilty. Guilt producing is a favorite technique for belittlers, for in addition to providing the status differential they seek, it also makes them feel non-accountable.

"It's all your fault" has an even darker side, when it appears in a slightly different context: "You should have listened to me when I told you not to marry him. Now you can blame only yourself!" The blamer's sanctimoniousness and seemingly superior wisdom are sure to make the target, who has already been hurt, feel stupid, as well. Children are particularly at risk when they are repeatedly subjected to such "I told you so" attacks (see pp. 122–123 in Chapter 7), for instead of acquiring the Eriksonian virtue of initiative, they become inhibited, unable to plan or to achieve goals (Carr, 2006, p. 38).

You're oversensitive

This frequently heard sentence tends to come up during interpersonal altercations. Our clients often quote it as having been said by their partner who is reluctant to come to therapy. It is also used against children who have been hurt physically or emotionally. One participant is insulted, expresses hurt, pain, verbal or non-verbal anger, and the other reacts by an accusation: "You're making a mountain out of a molehill"; "you're too emotional"; "you're exaggerating!" By using this ploy, the belittler releases self from responsibility for the harm done, and places a double burden on the other: in addition to the initial insult, s/he is now told that s/he suffers from a character defect. The source, in turn, gains twice, by hurting without owing up, and by being depicted as the rational, balanced party.

The belittling that takes place here has a guilt producing element, as well. The target may hesitate: "Perhaps I did overreact? Am I being too emotional?" The entire situation is based on a power differential, where the belittler enjoys a higher status than the one on the receiving end.

There are several possible motives behind this saying.

1. The source cannot cope with a display of emotions. The capacity to accurately interpret and deal with others' emotions is a basic component of Emotional Intelligence (see Goleman, 1995, p. 43).
2. This incident reminds the source of his or her own difficulty to deal with emotions (this is another component of Emotional Intelligence).
3. Unable to cope with criticism, the source turns the tables on the target.
4. In the ongoing struggle between the two parties, the source uses every opportunity to gain an upper hand.

Underlying any criticism that deals with one's supposed "exaggerating" is the question, who has the right to decide? Who is in a better position to measure the appropriateness of a response than the respondent? Whenever we come across a response that appears to us to be an overreaction, we need to ask ourselves: what nerve have we touched and what unfinished business lies behind this reaction? Respecting, rather than belittling the other person, listening to him or her empathically, will lead to an I-message: "I see that you're hurt. I'm willing to talk about this."

But the insult hidden in this saying does not end here. There is an additional voice there, saying: "Change, conform, don't feel what you feel, don't wish what you wish!" Any statement criticizing one's being different (in feelings, thoughts, behaviors, needs or wishes) belittles one's right to be unique, demands to fall in line with the rest. Instead of listening to one's concerns, the message is: Change! This is the conditional positive regard, decried by Rogers (1990b), where I'll accept you only if you fit yourself to *my* needs.

Activities

1 A word to the wise

See Activity number 1 in Chapter 5.

2 Little people

This is a guided imagination activity.

Trigger: Darken the room, speak slowly, in a relaxed, low voice: Sit in a comfortable position, close your eyes, breathe deeply. Think of an event in your family where you felt small, smaller than you usually think you are. [pause] Who gave you this feeling? How was it given? [pause] What was your reaction? [pause] What would you have needed to feel comfortable in that situation? [pause] Breathe deeply, move your limbs, open your eyes slowly. Turn on the lights.

Invite the family member who made you feel small and talk to him or her, without blaming, using congruent communication and I-messages. [be on guard and stop/correct dysfunctional utterances] Think of situations where you have belittled others. How does it feel? Send a different message that does not hurt the other person.

3 Pick a card

Trigger: Prepare index cards with such sentences printed on them as "I know better what's good for you!"; "You'll understand when you grow up"; "Why can't you see this?"; "No wonder they ask for my advice and not yours"; "You really know nothing about education"; "Don't forget who earns the money in this family!"; "The children love my parents more than they love yours!" (add more or write others that fit the family). Add some blank cards.

Read the cards and take one that is relevant to your family. You can write your own, if you wish.

Possible points for discussion:

Share the reasons for choosing this card.
How does this saying affect you and where does it place you in the family?
What are the costs and benefits of this saying for you as an individual and for the family unit?

Hold a dialogue with the source of the saying, using congruent communication. (Other family members are invited to intervene when communication becomes dysfunctional.)

4 Family sculpture

Trigger: One of the family members "sculpts" the others by placing them in various characteristic positions at meaningful distances from each other. They can face or be back to back, touch, stroke or strike, kneel, lie down, open their mouth for a scream – anything the sculptor deems necessary. The result is a typical 3D picture of the family. Now the sculptor stands behind each in turn, and gives them a single sentence, which s/he finds most characteristic of that person. Each family member repeats this sentence aloud. The sculptor may correct stances or utterances, then enter the picture him/herself. Family members alternate at looking at the sculpture, while the therapist takes their place and sentence.

Possible points for discussion:

What do you feel when you look at the family sculpture?
How does this family structure benefit some family members and at what
    cost?
Which of these sentences makes you feel an equal, and which belittles you?

5 Ruler

Trigger: Give each person a crayon and a page with a vertical ruler drawn on it. Think of a moment when you felt uncomfortable within your family. Mark on the ruler the spot that indicates the "height" of each family member at that moment (including yourself). Hand out a different crayon. Now think of a pleasant moment within your family, and mark each member's "height" on that occasion.

Possible points for discussion:

Notice the differences in height at good vs. bad moments.
How is belittling connected to those feelings?
What changes can you make to have more positive than negative moments?
What have you learned about yourself and about your family today?

9

Bookkeeping, or Just You Wait

> For her part, she had invested everything in love . . . ; in turn, she had
> expected her partner to invest an equal capital of feelings in the common
> account. To redress the imbalance, she gradually withdrew her emotional
> deposit and after the wedding presented a proud, severe face to her husband.
> (Kundera, 1986, p. 5)

Social psychologists and sociologists have developed robust theories
concerning the initiation and maintenance of interpersonal relationships.

*Destructive Myths in Family Therapy: How to Overcome Barriers to Communication by Seeing and
Saying – A Humanistic Perspective*, First Edition. Daniela Kramer-Moore and Michael Moore.
© 2012 John Wiley & Sons, Ltd. Published 2012 by John Wiley & Sons, Ltd.

Notable among these are the theories of *social exchange* and of *social equity*. According to the former, we look for ties in which we can maximize our net gains. Research shows that this social-emotional profit seeking takes into account two additional variables: what we think we deserve, and what our alternatives are (Le and Agnew, 2003). Equity theory goes one step further by suggesting that we enter into the equation our partner's outcomes, as well, and prefer equitable relationships to inequitable ones: we especially dislike being under-benefited, that is to say, getting less out of a relationship than our partner does (Guerrero, La Valley, and Farinelli, 2008). Both of these theories consider even the most intimate relationships as analogous to the trading of goods at a marketplace (see also Scanzoni's concept of reward-seeking in his 1972 treatise on sexual bargaining). And, as much as we may bristle at the thought, empirical evidence supports the idea that we all engage in some rudimentary bookkeeping. Box 9.1 provides more information on models of social interaction.

Box 9.1 Self-interest or altruism?

Economic models of behavior usually assume a more-or-less rational, self-interested actor. How reasonable is this assumption?

Altruism is usually defined as the intentional, yet unrewarded helping of others; some will add that in order to be called altruistic, an act must also be costly to the helper, that is to say, it must increase another's chances of survival at the expense of one's own. Arguably, the world would be a better place if altruism flourished, yet many social scientists dispute its very existence in human behavior.

Jensen (1998), for instance, found it "inconceivable that purposeful action on the part of human beings can be viewed as anything other than responses to incentives. Indeed, the issue of incentives goes to . . . the very core of what it means to choose. Rational individuals always choose the option that makes them better off as they see it" (p. 40). Jensen then went on to say that some behaviors that seem to be irrational and inconsistent with self-interest can also be explained if one postulates a "pain avoidance model": "While attempting (generally subconsciously) to avoid pain associated with recognizing personal

(continued)

error, people often put themselves in a position where they incur far more pain" (p. 43). Such behavior, we suggest, is certainly short-sighted, even blind, but it is also rational and self-serving at the moment it occurs. As for pure altruism – Jensen denied that it exists. Instead, he suggested that the altruistic acts people perform occur side by side with, as well as altered by, acts of self-interest.

The model developed by Piliavin and her colleagues (e.g. Piliavin, 2008) is just as explicit in its analysis of altruism, better labeled as pro-social or helping behavior. In this cost/reward model four elements are taken into account: the cost and the benefit of helping, as well as the cost and the benefit of withholding help in a specific situation. Only when the balance of these four inputs is positive (i.e. the sum of benefits exceeds the sum of costs), will a helping act be offered. When applying this model it is important to keep in mind that costs and benefits need not be material: they can include such intangibles as appreciation received from others, the relief of tension, the fear of guilt feelings, and even one's believed share in the hereafter. Research reported by Piliavin (2008) suggests that "doing good" is positively related to psychological well-being and self-reported health. We can therefore conclude that helping others can be in one's self-interest!

Yet, in spite of its ubiquity and possible usefulness, bookkeeping creates a problem, especially when it is persistently applied within an intimate relationship. Individuals whose main concern is "looking out for number one" enter such associations distrusting the other participant(s) and make cooperation very difficult. Homo Economicus as we may be, our spousal, parental, or simply comradely relationships are better served if we regard them as team effort, rather than competition. (Read more about competition vs. cooperation in Chapter 10).

Individualism vs. Collectivism

Profoundly different modes of social interaction form the basis of a fundamental division between two types of societies: those driven by collectivism, as opposed to those founded on individualism. In the former, individuals regard themselves as part of some aggregate (family, tribe, nation), whose norms direct their behavior. Members of the latter are largely independent individuals, whose behavior is rooted in personal goals and norms (see, for example, Dwairy, 2006; Dwairy and Van Sickle, 1996; Triandis, 1995). Triandis (1991, p. 87) pointed out that the importance attached to hierarchy (see Chapter 7 on inequality) must also be considered: collectivists overemphasize its role in society, while individualists pay it too little attention. One might expect more widespread competitiveness, with concomitant bookkeeping, among individualists, yet empirical data seem to say otherwise: instead of social climbing, collectivists tend to compete both across entire cultures, and within their social unit or stratum. Neither is there any evidence for less bookkeeping in collectivistic societies; it is abundantly present in cultures as different from each other as the Dobu Islands (practising *wabuwabu*, or "a system of sharp practices which stresses one's own gains at the expense of another's loss"; Fromm, 1977, p. 239) and Japan (whose culture includes *On*, signifying "the unlimited debt of gratitude or obligation of the recipient to the bestower of . . . grace"; Reischauer, 1977, p. 141; see also Moore & Kramer, 2000, on bookkeeping in religions).

Bookkeeping in the Family

Marriage is a long-term emotional, sexual and economic contract. Partners to this, as to any contract, prefer at least an equitable, if not a profitable deal. The fear of being the one with the lower hand drives each partner to a defensive stance. Throughout the life of the contract, they try to guard their rights, making sure they are not exploited. To this end they must do some elementary bookkeeping, or a count of investments and returns. The principle underlying this activity was referred to as "the balance of equitable fairness" by Boszormenyi-Nagy and Ulrich (1981). These founders of *Contextual Family Therapy* regarded such balancing as the cornerstone of their therapeutic approach. They emphasized that "fairness" does not involve some mechanistic, rigid bartering system but rather "the long-term preservation of an oscillating balance among family members": every person's interests are equitably safeguarded. Most couples seen in therapy have not reached the understanding that successful spousehood is based on such balanced cooperation (a parallel, rather than either complementary or symmetrical relationship; see Chapter 2). Instead of the free flow of sharing and teamwork, each partner stands on guard, "gives" in order either to "receive" or to enjoy the creditor's position. Constant bookkeeping destroys any sense of togetherness.

In his discussion of contextual family therapy Carr (2006, pp. 163–164) stressed the transgenerational aspects of bookkeeping: "For each family member, each family relationship entails an unconscious ledger of accumulated accounts of entitlements and debts that reflects the balance of what has been given and what is owed. When there is a significant imbalance in such ledgers, across generations, problems may occur . . . . therapists disrupt the intergenerational transmission of destructive interaction patterns . . . ." Children learn this mode of coexistence from their parents and practice it with their siblings: Who got more? Who hasn't done their fair share of the chores? When bookkeeping takes place between parents and children, the former remind the latter of all that they have done for them, demanding a repayment of old debts. They may also be willing to bribe their children with material goods, in return for their continued affection.

The sayings that follow vary in their directness: Some encourage bookkeeping openly, others must be looked at carefully to locate the insidious message they contain.

You owe me!

You can hear this coming from parent to child, from spouse to spouse, from sibling to sibling. "You owe me!" must be the purest illustration of bookkeeping. It differs from proper accountancy only in the currency required to settle an account. Instead of asking one's debtor to pay a dozen pieces of gold, creditors may ask for some work to be done (ranging from "take out the garbage" to "now it's your turn to change grandpa's diaper") or they may expect even less tangible goods, such as love, respect, or at least obedience. When angry parents come to family therapy with a child who has been caught (say, for truancy, shoplifting, or drugs), sooner or later they will say: "After all we've done for him . . . " The underlying message is that a contract has been broken. "We've fulfilled our part of the deal, why can't s/he do the same?" The child, however, may have a different perception of things. "I've nothing to be grateful for. I didn't ask to be born into this family. What you gave me was out of your free choice".

Though it is often parents who hold their children accountable, "You owe me" has a spousal version, too, as in "You should be grateful I married you (because of my wealth, looks, status or other qualities)." We do not deny the contractual nature of marriages, yet turning the relationship into a market place destroys intimacy and mutual respect. When one partner is reminded of his or her debts, s/he inevitably files a counter-suit: "Don't

think you were such a great catch. Here is a list of your deficiencies...."
The bickering that ensues is hardly conducive for a friendly relationship;
for in the contest that takes place each participant tries to build him/herself
up at the expense of the other.

So what went wrong in a family if a master financier is needed to keep
track of debts? First of all, the participants in such squabbles do not appear
to regard themselves as members of the same team. Naturally, even those
who cooperate fully with other members of their group are not expected to
contribute equally to the group goals at any given moment (see the concept
of oscillating balance, mentioned above). However, they do not need to
resort to bookkeeping. Being interested in each other's welfare – as well
as in their own – they can trust the others to pull their own weight when
necessary. This trust is another missing ingredient in many dysfunctional
relationships: "I've done things for you, and I don't trust you to repay me
on your own. So here is a reminder!" When there is no trust between two
members of the group, neither is there intimacy: "The capacity for affection,
warmth, closeness, etc., cannot be preserved if no honest effort is being made
to balance the ledger" (Boszormenyi-Nagy and Ulrich, 1981, p. 171).

I'll never forgive you

Families are sometimes regarded as small societies; societies have occasionally been analyzed as big families. This comparison of micro and macro is
useful up to a point, but, as is always the case with analogies, it can also be
misleading. Just as children learn that some things that are said and done
within the family circle are inappropriate outside their home, they also need
to realize that the rules of conduct laid down for public transactions are
not suitable for home usage. Now while parents are quick to insist on the
etiquette portion of this statement ("Be on your best behavior when we visit
your dad's boss!"), they often fail to follow its counterpart, thus bringing
home the rules of the office, the factory, or the church.

A particularly damaging example is the application to family life of
the cops-and-robbers mentality, unfortunately so necessary in some
contemporary societies. We, the authors of this book, along with some
of our readers, may dream of a society where more schools are built and
fewer prisons, where antisocial behavior is prevented, rather than either
punished or glorified, and where swords are beaten into ploughshares.
In his vision of what is possible to achieve through the application of
humanistic principles Rogers (1972) went as far as to draw the picture of

"the person of tomorrow," who will live and thrive in such a society (see p. 13 in Chapter 1; cf. Fromm, 1962, for his vision of the "New Man"). However, current realities necessitate powerful police forces that fight crime, and justice systems that mete out punishment. Notice that both of these estates subscribe to the saying under discussion: they never forgive.

Yet a family's emotional health is based on trust, respect, intimacy, and authentic communication, rather than on the suspicion, disregard, remoteness and manipulativeness so common in public life. (Cf. the similar issue of applying business rules to spousal relationship in "Play hard to get," in Chapter 6.) Parents punish their children instead of maintaining with them a dialogue about choices and consequences. Children, in their turn, learn not to abstain from, but to hide their offending behaviors. Not getting caught may in itself become a challenge, with energies of both the "cops" and the "robbers" being channeled into an unhealthy game. There are no winners, however. Whether the "criminals" are caught and punished or not, playing the game only increases estrangement and mistrust between children and parents. "Of course I read my daughter's diary, how else would I know what she's up to!" says this mother. "I never tell my parents anything personal, because they'll use it against me!" says her daughter.

Such intrusion of macro rules into micro environments can happen in spousehood, as well. Under the pretext of self-preservation husbands and wives can systematically hide from each other thoughts, emotions, behaviors, as well as material objects. If the situation demands it, they set traps for and spy on their marriage partner, not realizing that neither their self nor their marriage is preserved by adherence to norms perfectly acceptable in non-intimate environments.

"I'll never forgive you" is either a threat, intended to prevent what its author regards as a crime ("If you marry her, I'll never forgive you!"), or a punishment, once it has been committed ("I'll never forgive you for what you've just said!"). In either case, it tells its target that a book is being kept of his or her crimes; that these are neither forgotten nor forgiven and can be used against the offender at any time. But none of us likes to be threatened (chronically, in this case), so intimacy is harmed, hostility becomes entrenched. When one is afraid ("When will s/he bring it up?"), it is hard to build or maintain a trusting, sincere, and safe relationship. In the hierarchy of blamer and blamed that is created there is no room for constructively coping with the underlying conflict.

In family therapy we often find that once family members are confronted with the vicious circle that characterizes this saying, they start bargaining. "I won't forgive you, either," and "I'll forgive you this, if you forgive me that." There is a lot of resistance to open up and to let go of old grudges, because that entails a loss of one's bargaining position. Only when the costs of such unfinished business become clear can a gradual process of reconciliation start.

But you yourself have said so!

In this scenario the speaker exploits what the listener revealed (either about self or about somebody else) on a previous occasion. There must have been some closeness between the two, a degree of trust, for one of them to have said something authentic, to confess a regret, some doubt or weakness. Now there is a new situation, with the same players, in which one uses a past intimacy to either win some points or to make the other lose some. But the momentary victory creates subsequent losses, as is the case with other instances of mixing intimacy with bookkeeping.

Notice again how intimate and non-intimate situations demand different strategies. In a courtroom the prosecutor is entitled, indeed required, to use past confessions in an attempt to obtain conviction. And, that is the reason for procedures that protect individuals against self-incrimination in many countries. "Anything you do say may be given in evidence" is the caution given to suspects in England – should children, spouses, friends be also cautioned before opening their mouth in an informal conversation? Politicians are expected to be careful of what they say in public, for there might be a record made, which could be brought up on a later occasion. So perhaps one should make sure no notes are taken, no sound recording is made when one pours out one's heart to a trusted listener! All this may sound like an absurd exaggeration, but this is exactly the message sent by someone who abuses a past confidence. Receivers of the "I heard you saying"-type message are likely to be hurt, to feel angry and betrayed. Those among them who are able to benefit from experience will become more cautious in the future, probably generalizing their newly learned skill to other people, as well. Authenticity and congruence do not seem to pay, so they resort to either dissembling or to silence.

Parents who have done this to their children will then complain: "My son/daughter is not talking to me about anything significant!" A wife or a husband may find themselves in the same situation, noticing one day that their partner has stopped confiding. (Of course, other scenarios may be behind both a child's and a spouse's reticence.) They fail to realize that it was they who paralyzed the other by throwing at them a past indiscretion.

It serves you right!

Blaming the victim is an old ploy – its ancient roots are tied to the belief in a cosmic bookkeeper, who first notes and records every human act, then metes out their just deserts. For many believers, if not most, it logically follows that whatever happens to you must be a consequence of your past behavior (see, for example, verse 25 in *Psalms* 37: "I have been young and I have grown old, and I have never seen the righteous forsaken and their offspring begging for bread"). In modern times this logic has been used with the same facility for the justification of racial discrimination, genocide, and rape (BBC, 2010; Ryan, 1976), as well as for an explanation for life threatening diseases (e.g. cancer, in Lobchuk et al., 2008). The belief behind "It serves you right" has many popular forms, such as "what goes around, comes around"; "every dog's day comes"; and "you reap what you sow," based on a verse from the New Testament, expresses the same notion. Social psychologists relate this well-researched, cross-culturally generalizable concept of a *belief in a just world* (correlated with religiousness and authoritarianism in Rubin and Peplau, 1975 and reviewed by Furnham, 2003), to a more general construct, namely the illusion of control. After all, if good deeds are followed by rewards, and bad ones by punishment, one is able to control one's destiny! While this belief has some positive aspects and may serve as a mechanism for coping with the harsh realities of life, it can also lead to self-blame: "I must've done something bad to deserve this!" When abused children or spouses reach this conclusion, it becomes extremely hard for them to complain or to break out from their noxious relationship.

Picture the situation in which someone has been told "It serves you right." Something bad or unpleasant has happened to this person, some emotional or physical harm has occurred. When s/he shares this distress with another, instead of empathy, s/he gets a slap in the face: whatever has happened to you, you've got only yourself to blame. Even if the target of this saying does not share the belief in a just world (which would lead to self-blame), s/he is left alone, abandoned by someone whom s/he has trusted. Whether played out in the family, between or within generations, among friends, or in the workplace, this scenario leads to distance and mistrust, undermines intimacy, blocks communication. The target is likely to conclude: "Better to conceal my future failures and failings, for I haven't gained anything by revealing this one."

This is the last time I'm taking you on an outing!

Here the source uses a threat to remind its target of the book that is being kept of the latter's alleged transgressions. Threats are coercive techniques, based on some power differential between threatener and threatened: "Unless you behave as I demand, I'll make something unpleasant happen to you!" How successful threats are is not entirely clear. A study by Kellermann and Shea (1996) suggested that they are less efficient than direct requests, and no more efficient than promises. This is hardly surprising, since the threat vs. promise distinction is analogous to the much researched punishment vs. reinforcement issue. The latter have been consistently found more efficient than the former (Gonzalez-Mena, 2008, p. 126–129; see Box 9.2 for a clarification of what constitutes reinforcement as opposed to punishment). "Spare the rod and spoil the child" turns out to be a poor policy.

Box 9.2 On carrots and sticks

Before deciding whether to use reinforcement or punishment for changing someone's behavior, it is necessary to distinguish from each other four procedures: positive and negative reinforcement, and positive and negative punishment.

Reinforcement, as its name implies, is always applied with the intention to encourage the continuation of some ongoing behavior.

- In *positive reinforcement* this is done by rewarding the behavior that is desirable to the reinforcing agent. So if you want your adolescent daughter to share her thoughts with you, you could try some empathic listening when she starts talking to you, or even reciprocate by telling her something about yourself (assuming, of course, that she considers the latter a reward).
- *Negative reinforcement* is achieved when performing the desired behavior results in the removal or cessation of an aversive stimulus. So perhaps you could switch off the television, put away your

(continued)

newspaper, or stop talking on the phone and so encourage your spouse who comes home to tell you about his or her day! Again, some assumptions are necessary: you must be interested in your spouse's day, and s/he must dislike your customary inattention.

As opposed to reinforcement, punishment is always aimed at stopping some behavior.

- In *positive punishment* the unwanted behavior is immediately followed by something physically or psychologically unpleasant. Hitting, shouting at, shaming or mocking a child when s/he fails at school would be common examples of this type of behavior modification. Punishment has many negative side effects. One of them concerns not knowing what is considered reinforcement by the target person: it is not unusual for a child to obtain much needed attention by misbehaving; here instead of positive punishment s/he receives positive reinforcement.
- *Negative punishment* occurs when the unwanted behavior results in the removal of something an individual likes or wants. Spouses have been known to punish their partner for some offence by refusing sexual intimacy; parents often punish their children by the withdrawal of various privileges (TV time, pocket money, etc.).

Another method that can result in behavioral change is the withholding of any response (referred to as *extinction* by learning theorists). Consistently ignoring (that is to say, neither rewarding/reinforcing nor punishing) a child's temper tantrum falls into this category.

Regardless of success rate, the use of threats is an unwelcome behavior in a family setting, because it implies that the more powerful participant cares more for getting his or her way than for the other's physical or psychological well-being. When a threat becomes an empty threat, further problems arise. Consider the mother who yells at her son: "If you keep this up, I'll stop the car and you can walk home!" (There are many variations on this theme, such as "This is the last time I take you to a restaurant!"; "If you don't pick up your toys, I'll throw them in the garbage!"; "That's it – I'm getting rid of the TV!"). Targets of empty threats quickly discover that there is no follow up, and the resulting tendency to ignore the threats may easily generalize to ignoring the source (in this case, a parent) altogether. Another possible outcome gainsays the basic tenet that introduced this part of the book (*say what you mean and mean what you say*), and prevents both source and target from becoming aware of real needs and from practicing congruent communication.

Threats (empty or not) are not limited to the parent/child nexus. When they appear in spousal relationships they emphasize the power differential between the partners: The threatener controls some resources, while the threatened must be deserving in order to obtain them. Egalitarian communication, intimacy and affection are gone.

Activities

1 A word to the wise

See Activity number 1 in Chapter 5.

2 The black book

This is a guided imagination activity. Darken the room, speak slowly in a relaxed, low voice: Sit in a comfortable position, close your eyes, and breathe deeply. Think of the fights you have with a family member, and the things you can't "forget or forgive" this person, the things you tend to mention on such occasions. Now imagine you have a "black book" – open it and write these things down. [pause] Now on the opposing page list the things your partner to such fights usually brings up. [pause] When you're ready, open your eyes slowly. Turn on the lights.

Possible points for discussion:

What are the short and long-term gains and losses of keeping such a "virtual" book?
Does keeping such a book help you as an individual?
Does it help you as a member of the family?
What would you need to put these things aside?

3 Rooms

Trigger: Draw a house with many rooms. Give each room the name of a family member. Look at each room and check: Do you have some unfinished business with this person? Are there any outstanding emotional debts between you?

Possible points for discussion:

Choose a family member with whom you can now discuss the effects of such bookkeeping.
What do you gain and lose by keeping the book open?
What is needed to close the book?
Talk about how you can turn this unfinished business into a jumping board toward better communication.

4 Family secrets

Trigger: Each member of the group receives an envelope. Put inside the envelope your private and family secrets, and seal it. The contents will not be revealed at any time, unless you choose to do so.

Possible points for discussion:

Which of these secrets serves as a "weapon" against another family member?
Do any of these secrets cause debts?
What are the costs and gains of keeping secrets?
What would happen if they came out?
Sort (in your head) those that are kept secret due to the need for privacy, from those due to guilt or shame.
What's constructive about privacy?
What's destructive about guilt and shame?

5 Shopping list

Trigger: Each person receives a small notebook, allots a separate page to every family member, and makes a list of unfinished business s/he has with them.

Look at your notebook. Stop and reflect upon the gains and losses of having unfinished business. Discuss and share thoughts.

10

Family Rivalry, or Divide and Conquer

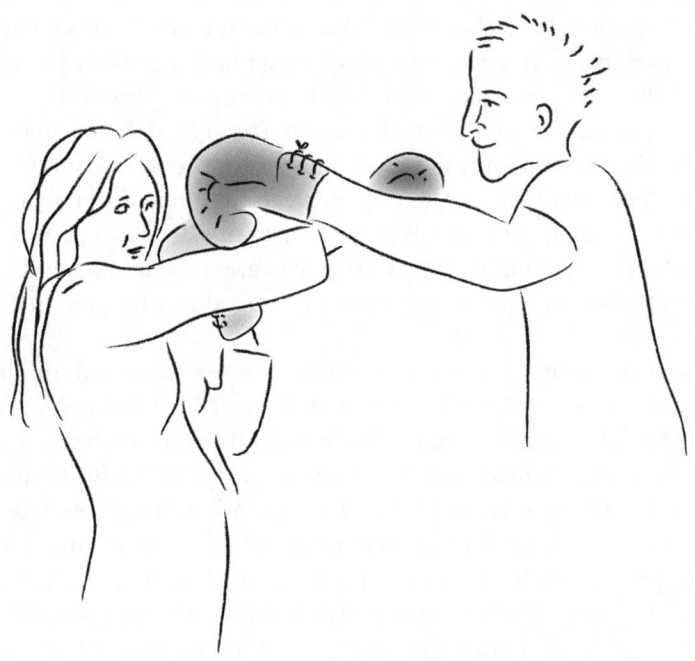

**Tell me, my daughters, – Since now we will divest us both of rule,
Interest of territory, cares of state, – Which of you shall we say doth love us
most? (Shakespeare, *King Lear*, I, p. i)**

When we started to write this chapter we thought we would devote it to
sibling rivalry. We soon realized that there was much to be said about
rivalry within families that extended beyond siblings: rivalry between the

---

*Destructive Myths in Family Therapy: How to Overcome Barriers to Communication by Seeing and
Saying – A Humanistic Perspective*, First Edition. Daniela Kramer-Moore and Michael Moore.
© 2012 John Wiley & Sons, Ltd. Published 2012 by John Wiley & Sons, Ltd.

parents, between parents and children, or between families of origin, just to mention a few. It is worth examining the source of the word *rival*. It designates the person on the opposite side of the river, and reminds us of the potential enmity between neighbors who compete for a scarce resource. Such competitiveness is an age-old characteristic of all living organisms. In human affairs, we can safely attribute to Heraclitus, the sixth century BCE philosopher, the view that competition is the driving force of every human activity. It was he who declared that "War is the father of all"; his interpreters have glossed this as referring to strife, conflict or opposition. Throughout the ages this view has had many followers who emphasize the positive aspects of competitive endeavors. It may even be argued that competition is a survival skill. It is not only the lower animals (or prehistoric humans) that fight over food, territory, and mating privileges; at times of scarcity in any of these resources many of us are likely to do the same. Our competitive streak can be observed both in infants' rivalry for parental attention and in such adult enterprises, as sport tournaments and auctions, where competition is the basic rule.

An opposite point of view is presented by those who regard competition as a destructive force. Karen Horney (1937), a neo-Freudian psychoanalyst, described a neurotic as someone who "constantly measures himself against others, even in situations which do not call for it" (p. 160). Alfie Kohn (1992, pp. 24–33), a well-known critic of current educational practices, found that far from being an inevitable part of human nature, competition is a learned phenomenon, a result of nurture, rather than of nature. Michael Argyle (1991, p. 4), one of the best known British social psychologists, was of the same opinion, further suggesting that cooperation is not only the cornerstone of many task-oriented activities (where coordinated effort can achieve goals no individual can achieve alone), but can also serve emotional goals, such as the enjoyment of joint activity or the furthering of a relationship. In their introductory chapter to a recent volume on cooperation, Sullivan, Snyder, and Sullivan (2008) also extolled its virtues: "Research across the social sciences is converging on the conclusion that a key ingredient for happy, well-functioning, and productive individuals and groups involves strong connections (characterized by fair treatment, trust, and mutual support) with other individuals, groups, and institutions. . . . At the heart of this convergence of research findings lies a deceptively simple, yet vitally important phenomenon – cooperation."

Instead of arguing whether competition is innate or acquired, and whether cooperation is the panacea for families, let us agree that both can be useful under certain conditions, and that we are all, at least theoretically, capable of both. Then the question arises – should families be run as sport events and commercial undertakings, or should they adopt the principles which help teams to achieve their goals? Some basic concepts from game theory, appearing in Box 10.1, will help answering this question.

Box 10.1   The games people play

"Game theory is the logical analysis of situations of conflict and co-operation" (Straffin, 2004, p. 3). The word "game" need not be taken literally; the theory applies to poker, chess, and tennis as well as to marriage, politics, and war. Myerson (1991, p. 1) suggested that a more descriptive name would be "'conflict analysis" or "interactive decision theory." In their simplest form, games are played by two parties. A central distinction game theory makes is between zero-sum and non-zero-sum games. In two-person zero-sum games one individual always does better at the other's expense, so that the sum of gains and losses is zero. No wonder such games are also called *strictly competitive*. A different type of interaction between two parties takes place in non-zero-sum activities; because of their overlapping interests, here it is possible for both participants to win (or to lose). Winning includes the enjoyment of an activity, such as experienced by children building sandcastles or playing with a ball.

The family context has endless examples of both types of games. The belittlers we met in Chapter 8, for instance, are all playing a zero-sum game: their sense of power is achieved through the weakening of another. Similar dynamics operate in symmetrical relationship (see Chapter 2), where two persons (say spouses or siblings) are engaged in a constant struggle over who is better, who is worse. And how about the relentless bookkeepers in Chapter 9? Their version of the game is also competitive, but need not be exactly zero-sum, for as a rule (and similarly to most sport events) they do not care about their partner's gains as long as their own exceeds them.

As for non-zero-sum games – they require cooperating team members. Any activity within the family (or some other intimate group),

(*continued*)

with any number of participants, can be played in this manner: preparing dinner, wallpapering the living room, or planning and taking a vacation, just to mention a few. In a book titled *Nonzero*, Wright (2000) argued that cooperation, necessitated by non-zero-sum activities, has evolutionary aspects. Natural selection goes hand in hand with increased complexity, and the latter demands increasing levels of cooperation and trust among individuals. According to Wright (2000, pp. 5–6) "Interactions among individual genes, or cells, or animals, among interest groups, or nations, or corporations, can be viewed through the lenses of game theory... New technologies arise that permit or encourage new, richer forms of non-zero-sum interaction; then... social structures evolve that realize this rich potential – that convert non-zero-sum situations into positive sums. Thus does social complexity grow in scope and depth."

This Box is not about the evils of zero-sum activities. We should not forget that quite often cooperation (within a group) is but a means to competition (between groups), as is clearly evident from a close look at both political alliances and team sports (see Axelrod, 1997, ch. 6). Furthermore, some competitive games (in the widest sense of the word) can be very enjoyable activities, if it is not always the same party who wins, and they are not the only type of game played.

We can now observe a consistent picture that emerges whether we consider the work done by Kurt Lewin and his colleagues in 1939 on different group climates, Baumrind's analysis of parenting styles in 1991 (for both of these see Chapter 7), or Wright's conclusions regarding non-zero-sum activities in 2000: cooperation, teamwork, and democratic leadership make for healthier, better functioning groups than do competition, rivalry, and autocracy. We conclude with confidence that families adopting these styles and principles will have less conflict and friction, and that their members will be more satisfied than those conducted on opposite lines. A proviso is in order: these positive outcomes become possible only if the family in question is embedded in a supportive culture, itself subscribing, at least nominally, to similar principles (see the discussion of the *multicultural perspective* in Chapter 3).

Sibling Rivalry

It will be instructive to examine the motivation of parents who encourage rivalry among their children. In healthy families the children constitute a team of peers, engaged in both competition and cooperation. However, these intragenerational coalitions are demolished when a parent draws one child closer, at the others' expense (resulting from triangulation, or perhaps from an unsatisfactory spousal relationship or a transgenerational process). Parents, along with grandparents and teachers who practice favoritism, empower themselves by encouraging fraternal contest and comparison. The friendship between one's children may be threatening, with the parent asking: Am I needed at all? Setting the children against each other is a PFP. Previously tame fights between siblings now metamorphose either into bitter struggles for power/affection/attention, or into emotional withdrawal from the sibling coalition. Sibling rivalry reflects spousal rivalry, and destroys the possibility of the siblings providing support and true companionship for each other. The damage is long lasting, for it is the sibling subsystem that provides the first experience of intimacy between equals. Skills obtained in a healthy sibling coalition include functional communication, sharing of physical and emotional territory, the equitable dealing out of duties and privileges. Children of families with clearly defined boundaries between subsystems are more likely to be relaxed and friendly with their siblings, and have a better chance to form egalitarian, healthy spousehood. Parental favoritism and resultant sibling rivalry force family members to take on pathogenic roles (see Mikkelson, 2006). The family is split into unhealthy subsystems by envy, competition and the need to gain the upper hand.

Parental Rivalry

Rivalry between parents or spouses is at the basis of *symmetrical* relationships, where two partners are in a constant power struggle with regard to their abilities and activities (see p. 29). Although this might appear as a fight for equality, the basis of the incapacity to enjoy true teamwork is one-upmanship. Spousal rivalry does not go hand in hand with emotional intimacy. It prevents the sharing of pains and failures, for one must always gain points, retain the upper hand. Underlying these dynamics is individuals' need to prove themselves worthy; this may be achieved by belittling each other. The higher spouses' self-esteem, the less they need to demonstrate it to their partner through controlling and belittling. High self-esteem may be based on objective grounds (healthy structure and communication patterns in the family of origin, education, status, attractiveness) or on subjective ones (emotional adjustment, contentedness, inner tranquility). When couples are separated by an objective or subjective gulf, they soon turn into a non-egalitarian dyad, in which one member constantly tries to control the other. Another unhealthy solution is for one member of the dyad to yield, thus turning the relationship into a *complementary* one (see p. 29).

Let him have it!

When two siblings fight, some parents intervene (though *interfere* might be a better word) and take sides. They tend to prefer the younger, weaker child and expect the older one to relinquish his/her claim over the toy or territory of contention: "You're the older one, let him have it!" So (as we have asked on previous occasions), who gains from this command? Certainly not the stronger one, who (perhaps along with other siblings witnessing this mini-drama) interprets this intervention as a preference for someone else, while s/he is treated as a second-class citizen. And though the weaker one might not realize this, neither does s/he, for now there is proof of his or her weakness and need to be protected. Instead of developing healthy coping mechanisms, s/he learns that being considered pitiful entitles him/her to practically everything. Not only is the development of positive self-esteem at risk here, but also an appropriate perception of reality. That leaves the parents who, having stopped the fight, can say to themselves: "We're peacemakers," not realizing that they have just sown the seeds of bigger and bitterer covert competition.

When the weaker child is able to enlist a parent against a sibling, an inter-generational coalition is created. The results of this unhealthy alliance range from momentary ill feelings to life-long envy and hatred. But the damage is not limited to the sibling relationship. Having learned to use their weakness as a weapon these children – as well as some only-children who have no experience in coping and fighting with their siblings – grow up lacking empathy, seeing only their own needs. There is a strong likelihood that they will use the same technique in their spousehood, and will transmit it to some of their children. This may well throw some light on the pathogenic behavior of adult family members who perceive themselves as either physically or emotionally ill and expect others to yield to their demands. The resultant skewed marital relationship (see Chapter 2) is a hotbed for the growth of distortions, cover-ups, and pseudo-mutuality.

One might ask: "But what if the children cause serious harm to each other?" True, some fights have to be stopped, and the combatants separated, yet this can be done without taking sides. No less important is to show the children that talking is more efficient than fighting. Once parents become aware of the damage they cause to vital sibling coalitions, they may want to invest some energy into helping it grow. This is how Minuchin (1974, p. 54) summed up the principle underlying this topic: "The development of skills for negotiating with peers, learned among siblings, requires non-interference from parents."

OK – Who started it?

This is what the person in charge is likely to ask whenever siblings or class-mates are fighting: *Who started it?* What s/he really wants to know is, who is to blame, and who should be punished. This guilt producing utterance promises retribution for the guilty party. Trying to save their own skin (a healthy survival skill) by pointing a finger at the other is a solution, though one that is unlikely to work. In their own worldview, the "combatants" may be right, too: each is thinking of a different starting point for the conflict. Was it when I was an only child, loved and appreciated, and my sibling was born, stealing my rights? Or yesterday, when grandma hugged one of us? Or when my rival was praised for some outstanding academic/artistic/athletic achievement? Family bookkeeping is a complicated and lengthy affair. Every act is listed (whether consciously or not); the present fight and its outcome are just another item on the long list.

So why is the parent so anxious to assign blame? Here are some possibilities.

1. According to a universal myth, in every conflict one party is right, one is wrong; the intervening parent helps to perpetuate the myth by acting as the judge.
2. The parent has more control over family dynamics if there is a parent–child coalition than with a sibling coalition.
3. Similarly to many other parental behaviors, the tendency to blame has been transferred transgenerationally: having seen in childhood that someone was always blamed, this parent automatically reacts by blaming.

4. The fight between one's children resembles spousal fights. By justifying one of the siblings, this spouse projects his/her (unconscious) hope that s/he will also be declared the winner in a spousal conflict.

A variation on the theme of "Who started it?" contains no external authority figure, for this type of blaming game can be played in dyads, as well: "You started, no, you started." This may well be one of the origins of endless spousal bickering that never leads to insight or to the ability to see beyond the immediate problem.

Why can't you be more like your sister?

Another way of encouraging sibling rivalry is the frequent drawing of comparisons among them. Whether individuals can and should be compared to each other is the subject of a long standing debate within psychology; two contrasting points of view appear in Box 10.2.

Box 10.2 General laws or unique personalities?

The field of psychology has known many deep rifts: Behaviorism set itself against psychodynamic approaches, experimentalists and correlationists established two practically non-overlapping disciplines, and clinicians live in a world quite different from that of their non-clinical brethren. This last distinction is based on two very different approaches to the study of any phenomenon: a search for general laws and principles, as opposed to an interest in individual cases. The former pursuit is referred to as *nomothetic*, while the latter is usually called *idiographic*. Though the introduction of these terms into psychology is customarily attributed to the American psychologist Gordon Allport (one of the founders of personality psychology who emphasized individuals' uniqueness; see Allport, 1937), Hurlburt and Knapp (2006) showed that they were in use already at the end of the nineteenth century.

The goal of operations guided by nomothetic principles is generalization. When searching for laws of behavior, adherents to the nomothetic approach tend to report the average performance of groups of individuals. If it becomes necessary to consider a single individual's

(*continued*)

behavior, this is achieved by its comparison to the behavior of the group to which s/he belongs. The nomothetic approach is often used in both the physical and the behavioral sciences. A frequent application can be observed in intelligence testing. For instance, if someone's IQ is 132, only about 2.5 percent of this person's age group are likely to have higher scores. Other standardized tests, whether of specific abilities, academic achievement or personality, operate similarly. The interpretation of a person's test behavior is made possible only by inspecting the degree of its deviation from a norm.

Quite a different approach is taken by those subscribing to idiographic methods. Here it is assumed that each individual is unique; if a person's behavior is to be evaluated, it is best compared to his or her own behavior at an earlier time, or under differing conditions. The Q-sort technique used by Rogers (described in Chapter 6) serves as a good illustration of such an idiographic approach when it is used to assess the gap between a client's real and ideal self, or when it assesses a client's progress during therapy. The work done by many clinicians – be they psychiatrist, social workers, clinical psychologists or counselors – tends to be more idiographic than nomothetic, in that their main goal is to improve the well-being of a specific client, rather than to generalize to a group of individuals. (For some implications of using nomothetic vs. idiographic grading methods in education see Moore, 2003, pp. 46–49.)

Though these two widely different approaches are not often employed by the same person, it is important to realize that they have both greatly contributed to the common goal of psychologists. Lee Cronbach (1957), who was president of the American Psychological Association over half a century ago, called this goal social betterment, and expressed his hope that one day the two disciplines of psychology will ask for it in a single voice. More recently Fraenkel (1995) advocated an "idiothetic" combination of the two approaches by practitioners of family therapy.

Comparing one sibling's behavior to that of another delivers several Layer B messages.

1. You are not unconditionally accepted.
2. I do not appreciate (your) uniqueness.

3. You can do better.
4. I prefer your sibling(s).

The myth regarding the positive educational value of competition is discussed in the opening of this chapter. Parents and teachers accepting this myth encourage competition by setting positive role models for the individual, hoping for increased effort, better performance. They do not realize that comparisons of any sort can hurt the targets' self-confidence – that they belittle and frustrate. Try to empathize with them and ask yourself: What can one, who is constantly compared to a brother or sister, feel towards self, parent, and sibling? Disappointed at themselves, the targets of this saying are prone to become angry and to conclude that they cannot win this contest. So, in addition to the damage it causes, the comparison is unlikely to work as an effective means of control. The parents certainly do not endear themselves by declaring their preference for one or more of their other children. And, finally, those other, ostentatiously more successful siblings, instead of providing support and being part of a sibling coalition, become objects of envy.

Comparisons are practiced in the classroom, as well, either directly ("You should all look at the work Lucy has handed in!") or indirectly, through commonly used grading techniques, such as "grading on the curve" (Moore, 2003, pp. 39–44). It is not unusual for students, finding themselves unable to compete, to stand out from the crowd via disruptive or destructive behavior.

Children, who grow up not being appreciated for who they are, experiencing constant comparisons to others, are apt to adopt this style and use it toward their children and their spouse. To show how deficient they are, husbands and wives are compared to friends, neighbors, old flames. As with children, this creates bitterness, distance, reduces intimacy, prevents healthy, egalitarian communication between the spouses.

Who loves Mommy best?

Parents are expected to understand and satisfy their children's needs. This starts with physical needs, such as food and shelter, and goes on to psychological ones: love, warmth, emotional security, a feeling of worth, more or less paralleling Maslow's famous pyramid of needs (Maslow, 1970). A family that requires a small child to support its parents by cooking and cleaning for them would be regarded dysfunctional. Yet a whole set of conventional sayings reveal that this is quite acceptable at the emotional level.

Whenever King Lear's sins are discussed, the focus is on his abdication, rather than on the love test he held among his daughters, thus both setting them against each other, and causing two of them to produce dishonest, fawning flatteries.

Love tests may convey a variety of messages to the contestants:

1. love needs proof;
2. I shall love you only if you love me;
3. since one of you loves me more, the others must love me less;
4. love is a measurable commodity; and
5. I am emotionally so deprived that I rely on your love to fill my needs.

Children subjected to such tests find themselves in an upside down world, where parents' needs come first and must be satisfied by their own children. At the emotional level the child learns that in order to gain parents' acceptance and approval, it has to give them the central spot on stage, and to give up its own emotional needs in their favor. In the extreme case incest occurs, where children fill their parents' sexual needs, often under the pretext of love. We have come across a case of a "loving" mother who engaged in sexual acts and enjoyed pornographic movie nights with her primary school sons. In such a relationship the child cannot realistically refuse: parents are the only source of succor and survival. Then there is the temptation: the child becomes an important character, often the favorite child. The price paid for this special status is very high: Hall et al. (1989) reported that 50 percent of anorexic and bulimic patients admitted to an eating-disorder unit had suffered sexual abuse, compared to only 28 percent of patients admitted with other eating-disorder diagnoses. Pribor and Dinwiddie (1992) found that rates of anxiety disorders, major depression, and alcohol abuse and dependence were significantly higher in a group of women who had been victims of incest during childhood than in a comparison group. But even in situations that are less extreme, emotional incest may take place: emotional intimacy develops that would be appropriate for spousal relationships. The parent–child tie leaves no room for others and endangers the spousal dyad, though, of course, this is a chicken-and-egg situation; a parent's emotional neediness may itself be the result of unsatisfactory spousehood. In another scenario the parent's behavior has transgenerational roots, and now s/he continues the chain, by passing a dysfunctional behavior to the next generation.

Activities

1 A word to the wise

See Activity number 1 in Chapter 5.

2 Once upon a time

Trigger: Give each family member a page with the beginning of a story: "Once upon a time there was a kingdom where the King, the Queen, the princes and princesses [gender and number same as in this family] were all happy and content, except for one of the children, who was always different." Continue this story by describing the characteristics, moods and behaviors of this child.

Each family member completes the story; the endings are read out.

Possible points for discussion:

What did you feel and think when listening to the stories?
How is the story connected to your family?
Which role is yours?
What are the family's costs and gains from having a child who deviates from the family norms?

3 Family scripts

Trigger: Each person writes a short script (5–6 sentences) of a repetitive, irritating family scene. Here is an example:

MOTHER:　You don't leave the house without a sweater!
CHILD:　　But mom, I look awful in it!
FATHER:　It's not that cold outside.
MOTHER:　You always have to take his side! If he catches a cold, it's me who'll have to stay home with him!

In this script, the discussion would focus on the covert competition between the mother and the father over the role of the "good parent."

Select a script that contains overt or covert rivalry or competition, and have family members act it out. Encourage them to voice inner voices, expressing these emotional needs [or give them yourself] (I want to feel important; I need them to listen to me; I'm old enough to know what's good for me; don't control me; I also exist in this family; I need to mediate; I can't stand these fights; I feel redundant unless I control things; I must have the last word) and encourage them to discuss the short-term benefits and the long-term costs of this rivalry to the family.

Possible points for discussion:

What are each person's underlying needs?
Are they related to control, feeling important, proving self-worth, power struggles between parents or between a parent and the child?
Talk about anxieties, gains and losses: What is my value if I'm not obeyed? What do I lose by being constantly in control?

This is a good opportunity to ask the family to translate the above script into a congruent one.

4 It figures

Trigger: Give each family member a page on which you have drawn several stick figures of different sizes. Add a text balloon to each figure. Label each figure as a member of this family, and write in the balloon a sentence that expresses this person's position in the family.

Possible points for discussion:

How do different positions in the family contribute to competition and feelings of rivalry?
What are the costs and benefits of not addressing the issue of rivalry within the family?

An alternative version: Supply crayons and ask family members to draw their family as stars of different size, shape, and color.

5 Family garden

Trigger: Give colored crayons to participants and ask them to draw the family (including themselves) as flowers of different sizes.

Possible point for discussion:

How do you feel about your size and place within the family?
Who is tall, who is short?
Who overshadows whom?
Who has no room to grow?
Who supports whom?
What does each person gain and lose by having this size and this location?
What can be done to give each family member a comfortable size and location?
What have you learned about yourself and about the family?

11

In Lieu of Conclusion
Myths in the Service of Psychopathology

I think my quarry is illusion. I war against magic. I believe that, though illusion often cheers and comforts, it ultimately and invariably weakens and constricts the spirit. (Yalom, 1991, p. 154)

In many ways, this book is about myths, and our endeavor may be regarded as a form of myth criticism, following Harris (1992, p. 244), who listed as one definition of that method the "[C]riticism of attitudes and beliefs that heavily influence or control society." Myths – distorted beliefs and rigid adherences to pathogenic behavior patterns – have a lot to do with *seeing* and *saying*: *Saying* them to oneself and to significant others prevents both speaker and listener from *seeing* painful family processes. The ability of myths to influence emotions, thoughts and behaviors derives from the power differential between their sources and their targets: it is the powerful, the ones who have authority and control over resources who use myths to keep the powerless in line. The parent–child nexus – ideal for the transmission of personality defining information – is such a relationship. Parents have the power to provide their children with sanitogenic messages, as well as with pathogenic ones. The former are characterized by authenticity, flexibility and openness; the latter by incongruence, rigidity and opaqueness.

It is the transgenerational nature of PFPs that makes family therapy necessary. Adults who have been brought up on a steady diet of pathogenic myths cannot simply switch to a new language; before learning congruent communication and empathy skills, they have to unlearn an entire repertoire of dysfunctional communication patterns. To be able to do that, they must first *see* the pain that is inflicted on their family. Entrenched beliefs resist attempts to change them; the difficulty is increased by myth holders' tendency to reject critical thinking (cf. Bowen's concept of *fusion* in Chapter 2). As a skilled observer of the family, the therapist is there to help family members recognize the costs and the transgenerational character of the myths they live with, and to begin questioning their validity. Here lies the importance of "stopping and reflecting," for once such questioning starts, it cannot be stopped.

Our brand of family therapy is not alone in pointing out the dangers of false beliefs. Boscolo et al. (1987), for instance, suggested that in the Milan Systemic family therapy "families come in with 'maps' of what is going on and ... the therapist attempts to challenge or shift these 'maps'" (p. 19). These maps contain collective myths; the therapist draws the family's attention to these myths and attempts to help the family get rid of them in order to bring about changes in family behavior. Cognitive-behavior family therapy (reviewed by Dattilio and Epstein, 2005), attributes crucial importance to *schemas*, that is, "the ingrained beliefs of family members about individual and family functioning" (Dattilio, 2005, p. 15). When the family schemas are dysfunctional, the cognitive-behavioral family therapist's intervention involves their restructuring in order to "facilitate more adaptive functioning and harmonious family interaction" (Dattilio, 2005, p. 24).

The family maps, schemas or myths we are concerned with lie on a continuum. At one end we find relatively mild cases that cause some suffering and discomfort: "Men are from Mars . . . " is used as an excuse for a husband and father's virtual muteness at home, or "jealousy is a sign of love" for a mother's aggressive outbursts. At the other end there are extreme cases involving grievous bodily harm: The "mother who sacrifices everything for her child" lies at the basis of Munchausen Syndrome by Proxy (see Box 11.1).

Box 11.1   Baron Münchhausen rides again

Those suffering from Munchausen Syndrome (also known as Hospital Addiction Syndrome) pretend to have some serious disease, often submitting themselves to unnecessary hospitalization and surgery. This psychiatric disorder was named after an eighteenth century German baron, famous for telling tall tales about himself. A sinister variation of it is the Munchausen Syndrome by Proxy (MSBP; currently known as Fabricated and Induced Illness), where an adult repeatedly submits another person, usually a child, to needless medical interventions, occasionally causing illness so as to prolong and justify treatment. MSBP parents (in the vast majority of the cases, mothers) are often well educated and especially knowledgeable about the illness of the child. Many have some formal or informal medical education, are very friendly with the medical staff and, unlike most parents, feel at home in hospital. They remain unusually calm in view of their child's undergoing painful medical tests. In his description of MSBP Stirling (2007, p. 1027; see also Kramer-Moore, 2010) gave the following examples:

(*continued*)

- A mother takes her child to the doctor for frequent evaluations for sexual abuse, even in the absence of objective evidence or history of abuse.
- Mothers insist their children be treated for attention-deficit hyperactivity disorder although there is no evidence to make the diagnosis.
- A parent starves her child because she wrongly "believes" he has multiple food allergies.
- Physicians suspect an unusual hematologic disorder after a mother repeatedly and secretly bruises her child with a hammer.
- The parent purposely suffocates her child and kills him during a hospitalization for "apnea."

The power of the "devoted mother" myth is tremendous. Spouses, friends and neighbors are taken in; entire communities enlist to defend the apparently dedicated mother who sacrifices everything for her sick child's sake. Believing the opposite would betray a universal family schema, that is, that Mothers love their children and would never intentionally harm them. Then there is the case of Kathy Bush, first named mother of the year by Hillary Clinton, then charged with aggravated child abuse and fraud for unnecessarily submitting her 7-year-old daughter Jennifer to some 200 hospitalizations and 40 operations (Toufexis, 1996). She was found guilty of deliberately making her daughter sick by tampering with her medications.

Unlike other disciplines in the social sciences, psychology looks at the individual. The former point out many additional aspects of myths and their positive contributions: myths are important for keeping society together; they prevent chaos and provide for continuity. We decline to join the discussion about the costs and benefits of myths at the macro level, focusing, instead, on family myths and their effect on family members. Our clinical experience shows that some family myths cause distortion and blindness, they prevent insight and block functional, healthy communication. These myths originate in what was imprinted on clients in their families of origin, and they keep preventing critical thinking and creative coping with crises. Clinging to myths thwarts adaptation to changing circumstances that inevitably result from the changing needs of family members. The family therapist's task is to listen to these myths, empathically grasp what needs they serve, and what alternative behaviors they block, and to help clients acquire effective coping skills that make these myths unnecessary.

We could not cover in this book every frightful saying we would all hear if only we listened carefully. The brief selection we offer should suffice to alert readers, and through them their clients, to recognize the sentences we hated to hear as children, and not to repeat them. Therapists can help family members be creative, and put it differently, put themselves in the listeners' place, think how it impacts them, what scars it will leave on them. No doubt, we all make many mistakes while mastering these skills. Yet the ability to say, "Let me rephrase this," is the first step on the road to authentic speech and sanitogenic communication within the family.

Activities

1 A letter to myself

Trigger: Write yourself a letter: How did I see myself when I started on this journey, how and why did I change, how am I today? What do I expect for the future? You may include reflections about the shape the family was and is in. Share with the others whatever you feel comfortable with.

2 Family sculpture

Trigger: Each family member in turn "sculpts" the family (can use modeling dough instead of the real persons) twice: the way they appeared at the beginning of the therapy and now.

Possible points for discussion:

How has the sculpture of the family changed?
Give feedback to family members about the changes they made.
How would you like this sculpture to look in a year from now?

3 I and We

Trigger: Provide blank sheets of paper, crayons, journals that may be cut up, scissors, paste. On one half of a folded page each member of the family creates a picture of "I," and on the other half a picture of "We," by writing, drawing, pasting. Now open and compare the two parts.

Possible points for discussion:

How do you feel about the relationship between I and We?
Would you like to change something in the pictures?
Have there been changes in the family?
What are your hopes for the future regarding I and We?

4 Temperature taking

Trigger: Give each person a page with a thermometer drawn on it. Think of a moment where you were involved in a family conflict. Mark the temperature of the anger or pain you experienced regarding this conflict. Try to sum up the agendas behind it.

Possible points for discussion:

What has changed in the family's ability to communicate about this conflict?
Use congruent communication to describe your feelings about it.
What have you learned about yourself and your family by examining this
    conflict?

5 The road taken

Trigger: Place two chairs at a distance from each other, draw a chalk line (or use colored tape) between them, and label them with written signs: "Where I was at the beginning of therapy" and "Where I hoped to be by now." These signs refer to the therapeutic process. Stand at the point where you perceive yourself today. Look at the distance you've covered.

Possible points for discussion:

What made you choose your place along the line?
How do you feel about the places others placed themselves?
In what areas has the family made progress?
If therapy was to continue, what would you like to accomplish?
How do you feel about the road you've taken in these sessions?

6 Closure

Trigger: Give each family member colored crayons and a page with the axes of a graph drawn on it. Label each axis with three points: the horizontal axis with beginning, middle, and end of sessions; the vertical axis with positive, neutral, and negative attitude. Pick three colors and draw on the chart lines representing your progress (ups and downs) in three areas: your attitude toward your own self, toward other family members, and toward the problem that made you come to therapy. Mark significant positive and negative events during therapy as points on the chart.

Possible points for discussion:

How did the 3 lines on the chart affect each other?
How do you feel about the road you have taken through participating in these sessions?
Now that formal therapy is about to be over, what are your plans for making further progress within the family?

References

Ackerman, F., Colapinto, J. A., Scharf, C., Weinshel, M., and Winawer, H. (1991) The Involuntary Client: Avoiding "Pretend Therapy". *Family Systems Medicine*, 9, 261–266.

Allport, G. W. (1937) *Personality: A Psychological Interpretation*, New York: Holt.

Altman, I., Vinsel, A., and Brown, B. B. (1981) Dialectic Conceptions in Social Psychology: An Application to Social Penetration and Privacy Regulation. *Advances in Experimental Social Psychology*, 14, 107–160.

American Psychiatric Association (2000) *Diagnostic and Statistical Manual of Mental Disorders*, 4th edn, text revision. Washington, DC: American Psychiatric Association.

Anderson, D. M., Keith, J., Novak, P. D., and Elliot, M. A. (2009) *Mosby's Medical, Nursing, and Allied Health Dictionary*, 8th edn, St. Louis, MO: Mosby.

Argyle, M. (1991) *Cooperation – The Basis of Sociability*, London: Routledge.

Aristotle (1946) *Politics*, tr. by E. Barker. Oxford: Clarendon (Originally written ca. 400 BCE).

Arnold, F., Kishor, S., and Roy, T. K. (2002) Sex-selective Abortions in India. *Population and Development Review*, 28, 759–785.

Aronson, E., Wilson, T. D., and Akert, R. M. (2010) *Social Psychology*, 7th edn, Upper Saddle River, NJ: Pearson.

Arseneault, L., Cannon, M., Fisher, H. L., Polanczyk, G., Moffitt, T. E., and Caspi, A. (2011) Childhood Trauma and Children's Emerging Psychotic Symptoms: A Genetically Sensitive Longitudinal Cohort Study. *American Journal of Psychiatry*, 168, 65–72.

Avtgis, T. A. (1998) Locus of Control and Persuasion, Social Influence, and Conformity: A Meta-analytic Review. *Psychological Reports*, 83, 899–903.

Destructive Myths in Family Therapy: How to Overcome Barriers to Communication by Seeing and Saying – A Humanistic Perspective, First Edition. Daniela Kramer-Moore and Michael Moore.
© 2012 John Wiley & Sons, Ltd. Published 2012 by John Wiley & Sons, Ltd.

Axelrod, R. (1997) *The Complexity of Cooperation – Agent-based Models of Competition and Cooperation*, Princeton, NJ: Princeton University Press.

Baldry, A. C. and Farrington, D. P. (2000) Bullies and Delinquents: Personal Characteristics and Parental Styles. *Journal of Community and Applied Social Psychology*, 10, 17–31.

Bandler, R., Grinder, J., and Satir, V. (1976) *Changing with Families*, Palo Alto, CA: Science and Behavior Books.

Batsche, G. M. and Knoff, H. M. (1994) Bullies and their Victims: Understanding a Pervasive Problem in the Schools. *School Psychology Review*, 23, 165–175.

Baumrind, D. (1991) The Influence of Parenting Style on Adolescent Competence and Substance Use. *Journal of Early Adolescence*, 11, 56–95.

BBC (2010) Women Say Some Rape Victims Should Take Blame – Survey, 15 February, http://news.bbc.co.uk/1/hi/uk/8515592.stm (accessed November 10, 2011).

Becvar, D. S. and Becvar, R. J. (2009) *Family Therapy – A Systemic Integration*, 7th edn, Boston: Pearson.

Bennett-Levy, J. (2003) Reflection: A Blind Spot in Psychology? *Clinical Psychology*, 27, 16–19.

Bergman, I. (1983) Scenes from a Marriage, in *The Marriage Scenarios*, New York: Pantheon, pp. 1–202.

Berne, E. (1964) *Games People Play – The Psychology of Human Relationships*, New York: Grove Press.

Berne, E. (1980) *Transactional Analysis in Psychotherapy*, London: Souvenir Press.

Bettelheim, B. (1976) *The Uses of Enchantment*, New York: Knopf.

Boscolo, L., Cecchin, G., Hoffman, L., and Penn, P. (1987) *Milan Systemic Family Therapy – Conversations in Theory and Practice*, New York: Basic Books.

Boszormenyi-Nagy, I. and Ulrich, D. (1981) Contextual Family Therapy, in *Handbook of Family Therapy* (eds A. Gurman and D. Kniskern), New York: Brunner-Mazel, pp. 159–186.

Bowen, M. (1976a) Theory in the Practice of Psychotherapy, in *Family Therapy – Theory and Practice* (ed. P. J. Guerin), New York: Gardner Press, pp. 42–90.

Bowen, M. (1976b) Family Reaction to Death, in *Family Therapy – Theory and Practice* (ed. P. J. Guerin), New York: Gardner Press, pp. 335–348.

Bowen, M. (1978) *Family Therapy in Clinical Practice*, New York: Aronson.

Brazier, D. (1997) Introduction, in *Beyond Carl Rogers* (ed. D. Brazier), London: Constable, pp. 7–13.

Bushman, B. J. and Anderson, C. A. (2001) Is It Time to Pull the Plug on the Hostile versus Instrumental Aggression Dichotomy? *Psychological Review*. 108, 273–279.

Carducci, B. J. (2009) *The Psychology of Personality*, 2nd edn, Chichester: Wiley-Blackwell.

Carr, A. (2006) *Family Therapy – Concepts, Process and Practice*, 2nd edn, Chichester: Wiley.

Centers for Disease Control and Prevention (2011) Bullying among Middle School and High School Students – Massachusetts, 2009. *Morbidity and Mortality Weekly Report*, 60(15), 465–471.

Chao, R. K. (1994) Beyond Parental Control and Authoritarian Parenting Style: Understanding Chinese Parenting through the Cultural Notion of Training. *Child Development*, 65, 1111–1119.

Chase, N. D. (1999a) Preface, in *Burdened Children* (ed. N. D. Chase), Thousand Oaks, CA: Sage, pp. ix–xi.

Chase, N. D. (1999b) Parentification – An Overview of Theory, Research, and Societal Issues, in *Burdened Children* (ed. N. D. Chase), Thousand Oaks, CA: Sage, pp. 3–33.

Cheever, J. (1982) *The Stories of John Cheever*, Harmondsworth: Penguin.

Clarkson, P., and Mackewn, J. (1993) *Fritz Perls*, London: Sage.

Coale, H. W. (1999) Therapeutic Rituals and Rites of Passage – Helping Parentified Children and their Families, in *Burdened Children* (ed. N. D. Chase), Thousand Oaks, CA: Sage, pp. 132–140.

Cook, W. L. and Douglas, E. M. (1998) The Looking-glass Self in Family Context: A Social Relations Analysis. *Journal of Family Psychology*, 12, 299–309.

Cooley, C. (1902) *Human Nature and the Social Order*, New York: Scribner.

Cronbach, L. J. (1957) The Two Disciplines of Scientific Psychology. *American Psychologist*, 12, 671–684.

Dattilio, F. M. (2005) The Restructuring of Family Schemas: A Cognitive-Behavior Perspective. *Journal of Marital and Family Therapy*, 31, 15–30.

Dattilio, F. M. and Epstein, N. B. (2005) Introduction to the Special Section: The Role of Cognitive-Behavioral Interventions in Couple and Family Therapy. *Journal of Marital and Family Therapy*, 31, 7–13.

Domestic Violence Victimization (1998) *Trainer's Manual: Improving Health Care Response to Domestic Violence Victims*, San Francisco, CA: Family Violence Prevention Fund.

Dreikurs, R., Grunwald, B. B., and Pepper, F. C. (1982) *Maintaining Sanity in the Classroom*, 2nd edn, New York: Harper and Row.

Dwairy, M. (2006) *Counseling and Psychotherapy with Arabs and Muslims – A Culturally Sensitive Approach*, New York: Teachers College Press.

Dwairy, M. and Van Sickle, T. D. (1996) Western Psychotherapy in Traditional Arabic Societies. *Clinical Psychology Review*, 16, 231–249.

Eco, U. (1990) *The Limits of Interpretation*, Bloomington, IN: Indiana University Press.

Erikson, E. H. (1963) *Childhood and Society*, 2nd edn, New York: Norton.

Ermisch, J., Iacovou, M., and Skew, A. (2011) Family Relationships, in *Understanding Society: Early Findings from the First Wave of the UK's Household*

Longitudinal Study, www.understandingsociety.org.uk/ (accessed November 9, 2011).

Fincham, F. D. (2004) Communication in Marriage, in *Handbook of Family Communication* (ed. A. L. Vangelisti). Mahwah, NJ: Lawrence Erlbaum, pp. 83–103.

Focus on the Family (2005) www.focusonthefamily.com/ (accessed November 11, 2011).

Foley, D. (2003) The Method of Dialogue – Promoting Understanding between Hawaiians and Non-Hawaiians, in *Handbook of Conflict Management*, (eds W. J. Pammer and J. Killian), New York: Marcel Dekker, pp. 243–256.

Fraenkel, P. (1995) The Nomothetic-idiographic Debate in Family Therapy. *Family Process*, 34, 113–121.

Freud, S. (1955) Beyond the Pleasure Principle, in *The Standard Edition of the Complete Psychological Works of Sigmund Freud*, vol. 18. London: Hogarth Press, pp. 7–64. (Originally published 1920)

Freud, S. (1959) Inhibitions, Symptoms, and Anxiety, in *The Standard Edition of the Complete Psychological Works of Sigmund Freud*, vol. 20. London: Hogarth Press, pp. 77–172. (Originally published 1926)

Freud, S. (1961) The Economic Problem of Masochism, in *The Standard Edition of the Complete Psychological Works of Sigmund Freud*, vol. 19. London: Hogarth Press, pp. 159–170. (Originally published 1924)

Fromm, E. (1962) *Beyond the Chains of Illusion*, New York: Simon and Schuster.

Fromm, E. (1965) *Escape from Freedom*, New York: Avon. (Originally published 1941)

Fromm, E. (1977) *The Anatomy of Human Destructiveness*, Harmondsworth: Penguin.

Furnham, A. (2003) Belief in a Just World: Research Progress over the Past Decade. *Personality and Individual Differences*, 34, 795–817.

Galvin, K. M., Bylund, C. L. and Brommel, B. J. (2008) *Family Communication – Cohesion and Change*, 7th edn. Boston, MA: Pearson.

Gibney, P. (2006) The Double Bind Theory: Still Crazy-making After All These Years. *Psychotherapy in Australia*, 12(3), 48–55.

Giovannini, D. (1998) Are Fathers Changing? in *Women, Work and the Family in Europe*, (eds. E. Drew, R. Emerek, and E. Mahon), London: Routledge, pp. 191–199.

Glasser, M., Kolvin, I., Campbell, D., Glasser, A., Leitch, I., and Farrelly, S. (2001) Cycle of Child Sexual Abuse: Links between Being a Victim and Becoming a Perpetrator. *The British Journal of Psychiatry*, 179, 482–494.

Glew, G., Rivara, F., and Feudtner, C. (2000) Bullying: Children Hurting Children. *Pediatrics in Review*, 21, 183–190.

Golden, W. L. (1985) Resistance in Cognitive-behavior Therapy. *British Journal of Cognitive Psychotherapy*, 1, 33–42.

Goldenberg, H. and Goldenberg, I. (2008) *Family Therapy – An Overview*, 7th edn, Belmont, CA: Thomson Brooks/Cole.

Goleman, D. (1995) *Emotional Intelligence – Why It Can Matter More than IQ*, New York: Bantam.

Gonzalez-Mena, J. (2008) *Foundations of Early Childhood Education*, 4th edn, Boston, MA: McGraw-Hill.

Gordon, T. and Edwards, W. S. (1995) *Making the Patient your Partner: Communication Skills for Doctors and Other Caregivers*, Westport, CT: Greenwood Publishing Group.

Green, H. (1964) *I Never Promised You a Rose Garden*, New York: New American Library.

Green, R. (1998) The Deadly Embrace: An Approach to Abusive Relationships. *Group Analysis*, 31, 197–211.

Green, R., Collingwood, A., and Ross, A. (2010) *Characteristics of Bullying Victims in Schools*, Research Report DFE-RR001, NCSR, UK.

Grimm Brothers (1944) *The Complete Grimm's Fairy Tales*, New York: Pantheon.

Grogan-Kaylor, A. (2005) Corporal Punishment and the Growth Trajectory of Children's Antisocial Behavior. *Child Maltreatment*, 10, 283–292.

Guerin, P. J. and Guerin, K. B. (1976) Theoretical Aspects and Clinical Relevance of the Multigenerational Model of Family Therapy, in *Family Therapy*, (ed. P. J. Guerin), New York: Gardner Press, pp. 91–110.

Guerrero, L. K., La Valley, A. G., and Farinelli, L. (2008) The Experience and Expression of Anger, Guilt, and Sadness in Marriage: An Equity Theory Explanation. *Journal of Social and Personal Relationships*, 25, 699–724.

Gunty, A. I. and Buri, J. R. (2008) Parental Practices and the Development of Maladaptive Schemas. Annual Meeting of the Midwestern Psychological Association, Chicago, IL.

Hall, R. C., Tice, L., Beresford, T. P., Wooley, B., and Hall, A. K. (1989) Sexual Abuse in Patients with Anorexia Nervosa and Bulimia. *Psychosomatics*, 30, 73–79.

Harris, W. V. (1992) *Dictionary of Concepts in Literary Criticism and Theory*, New York: Greenwood Press.

Harter, S. (2002) Authenticity, in *Handbook of Positive Psychology*, (eds R. Snyder and S. J. Lopez), Oxford, UK: Oxford University Press, pp. 382–394.

Hawker, D. S. and Boulton, M. J. (2000) Twenty Years' Research on Peer Victimization and Psychosocial Maladjustment: A Meta-analytic Review of Cross-sectional Studies. *Journal of Child Psychiatry*, 41, 441–455.

Heider, F. (1958) *The Psychology of Interpersonal Relations*, New York: Wiley.

Hesketh, T., Lu, L., and Xing, Z. W. (2005) The Effect of China's One-child Family Policy after 25 Years. *New England Journal of Medicine*, 353, 1171–1176.

Hogg, M. A. and Vaughan, G. M. (2011) *Social Psychology*, 6th edn, Harlow: Prentice Hall.

Hollander, E. P. (1981) *Principles and Methods of Social Psychology*, 4th edn, New York: Oxford University Press.

Horney, K., (1937) *The Neurotic Personality of Our Time*, New York: Norton.

Hurlburt, R. T. and Knapp, T. J. (2006) Munsterberg in 1898, not Allport in 1937, Introduced the Terms "Idiographic" and "Nomothetic" to American Psychology. *Theory and Psychology*, 16, 287–293.

Jackson, D. D. (1981) The Question of Family Homeostasis. *International Journal of Family Therapy*, 3, 5–15. (Originally published 1957)

Jensen, M. C. (1998) *Foundations of Organizational Strategy*, Cambridge, MA: Harvard University Press.

Jones, E. E. and Gerard, H. B. (1967) *Foundations of Social Psychology*, New York: Wiley.

Juhnke, G. A., Granello, D. H., and Granello, P. F. (2011) *Suicide, Self-injury, and Violence in the Schools – Assessment, Prevention, and Intervention Strategies*, Hoboken, NJ: Wiley.

Kaffenberger, C., Gibb, D., and Murphy, S. (2002) A Model for Using Empathy In Counselor Education at George Mason University, in *Dimensions of Empathic Therapy*, (eds P. R. Breggin, G. Breggin, and F. Bemak), New York: Springer, pp. 101–115.

Kellermann, K. and Shea, B. C. (1996) Threats, Suggestions, Hints, and Promises: Gaining Compliance Efficiently and Politely. *Communication Quarterly*, 44, 145–165.

Kelman, H. C. (1958) Compliance, Identification, and Internalization: Three Processes of Attitude Change. *Journal of Conflict Resolution*, 2, 51–60.

Kerr, M. E. and Bowen, M. (1988) *Family Evaluation*, New York: Norton.

Kohn, A. (1992) *No Contest – The Case Against Competition*, rev. edn, Boston: Houghton Mifflin.

Kohut, H. (1971) The Analysis of the Self – A Systematic Approach to the Psychological Treatment of Narcissistic Personality Disorders. *The Psychoanalytic Study of the Child*, Monograph No. 4. New York: International Universities Press.

Kohut, H. (1978) The Psychoanalyst in the Community of Scholars, in *The Search for Self – Selected Writings of H. Kohut*, New York: International Universities Press.

Kramer, D. and Moore, M. (2001a) Family Myths in Romantic Fiction. *Psychological Reports*, 88, 29–41.

Kramer, D. and Moore, M. (2001b) The More it Changes . . .: Gender Roles, Romantic Fiction and Family Therapy. *Psycoloquy, an APA sponsored Electronic Journal*, 12(24), www.cogsci.soton.ac.uk/cgi/psyc/newpsy?12.024 (accessed November 11, 2011).

Kramer-Moore, D. (2010) A Mother Won't Harm her Child – Children as Victims of the Munchausen-Syndrome-By-Proxy. Poster presented at the 5th

International Conference on Child and Adolescent Psychopathology. Roehampton University, London.

Kramer-Moore, D. and Moore, M. (2002) *Life Imitates Art – Encounters between Family Therapy and Literature*, New York: Solomon Press.

Kramer-Moore, D. and Moore, M. (2003) Pardon Me for Breathing: Seven Types of Apology. *Et Cetera - A Review of General Semantics*, 60, 160–169.

Kramer-Moore, D. and Moore, M. (2005) *Positive Conflict Resolution: A Workshop in Multi-cultural Empathy Training*, New York: Solomon Press.

Kundera, M. (1986) *Life is Elsewhere*, London: Faber and Faber.

Laurse, P. and Collins, W. A. (2004) Parent-child Communication during Adolescence, in *Handbook of Family Communication* (ed. A. L. Vangelisti), Mahwah, NJ: Lawrence Erlbaum, pp. 333–348.

Le, B. and Agnew, C. R. (2003) Commitment and its Theorized Determinants: A Meta-analysis of the Investment Model. *Personal Relationships*, 10, 37–57.

Lederer, W. J. and Jackson D. D. (1968) *The Mirages of Marriage*, New York: Norton.

Lee, E. (ca. 1910) Introduction, in *Essays by Sainte-Beuve*, London: Walter Scott, pp. vii–xviii.

Lewin, K. (1936) *Principles of Topological Psychology*, New York: McGraw-Hill.

Lewin, K. (1964) *Field Theory in Social Science*, New York: Harper.

Lewin, K., Lippitt, R., and White, R. (1939) Patterns of Aggressive Behavior in Experimentally Created "Social Climates". *Journal of Social Psychology*, 10, 271–299.

Lidz, T., Flack, S., and Cornelison, A. (1965) *Schizophrenia and the Family*, New York: International Universities Press.

Lietaer, G. (1997) Authenticity, Congruence and Transparency, in *Beyond Carl Rogers* (ed. D. Brazier), London: Constable, pp. 17–46.

Lobchuk, M. M., McClement, S. E., McPherson, C., and Cheang, M. (2008) Does Blaming the Patient with Lung Cancer Affect the Helping Behavior of Primary Caregivers? *Oncology Nursing Forum*, 35, 681–689.

Luft, J. (1969) *Of Human Interaction*, Palo Alto, CA: National Press.

Lyness, K. P., Haddock, S. A., and Zimmerman, T. S. (2003) Contextual Issues in Marital and Family Therapy: Gender, Culture, and Spirituality, in *An Introduction to Marriage and Family Therapy* (eds. L. L. Hecker and J. L. Wetchler), New York: Haworth, pp. 409–448.

Maccoby, E. E. (2007) Historical Overview of Socialization Research and Theory, in *Handbook of Socialization – Theory and Research* (eds J. E. Grusec and P. D. Hastings), New York: The Guilford Press, pp. 13–41.

Maddock, J. W. and Larson, J. W. (1995) *Incestuous Families: An Ecological Approach to Understanding and Treatment*, New York: Norton.

Martin, T. C. and Bumpass, L. L. (1989) Recent Trends in Marital Dysfunction. *Demography*, 26, 37–51.

Maslow, A. H. (1970) *Motivation and Personality*, 2nd edn, New York: Harper and Row.

Matson. F. W. (1986) Humanistic Political Science and Humane Politics, in *Politics and Innocence – A Humanistic Debate* (eds R. May, C. Rogers and A. Maslow), Dallas, TX: Saybrook, pp. 155–161.

McCollum, E. E. (1991) A Scale to Measure Bowen's Concept of Emotional Cutoff. *Contemporary Family Therapy*, 13, 247–254.

McCord, J. (1996) Unintended Consequences of Punishment. *Pediatrics*, 98, 832–834.

McGoldrick, M. and Carter, B. (2003) The Family Life Cycle, in *Normal Family Processes*, 3rd edn (ed. F. Walsh), New York: Guilford Press, pp. 375–398.

McGoldrick, M., Gerson, R., and Shellenberger, S. (1999) *Genograms: Assessment and Intervention*, 3rd edn, New York: W.W. Norton.

Mead, G. H. (1934) *Mind, Self, and Society from the Standpoint of a Social Behaviorist*, vol. 1. Chicago, IL: The University of Chicago Press.

Merikle, P. N. and Daneman, M. (1998) Psychological Investigations of Unconscious Perception. *Journal of Consciousness Studies*, 5, 5–18.

Metz, J. L. (2007) And They Lived Happily Ever After: The Effects of Cultural Myths and Romantic Idealizations on Committed Relationships. Unpublished Master's Thesis, Northampton MA: Smith College, http://dspace.nitle.org/bitstream/handle/10090/1001/MetzJordanaEntireThesis.pdf?sequence=1 (accessed November 11, 2001).

Mikkelson, A. C. (2006) Communication among Peers: Adult Sibling Relationships, in *Widening the Family Circle – New Research on Family Communication* (eds K. Floyd and M. T. Morman), Thousand Oaks, CA: Sage, pp. 21–35.

Miller, A. (1990) *For Your Own Good: Hidden Cruelty in Child-rearing and the Roots of Violence*, London: Virago.

Minuchin, S. (1974) *Families and Family Therapy*, Cambridge, MA: Harvard University Press.

Minuchin, S. and Fishman, H. (1981) *Family Therapy Techniques*, London: Tavistock.

Minuchin, S., Lee, W., and Simon, G. M. (1996) *Mastering Family Therapy – Journeys of Growth and Transformation*, New York: Wiley

Moore, M. (1978) An International Application of Heider's Balance Theory. *European Journal of Social Psychology*, 8, 401–405.

Moore, M. (1999) Problematic and Pathogenic Communication Patterns in Prayers. *Et Cetera – A Review of General Semantics*, 56, 192–203.

Moore, M. (2001) " This is Like Déjà Vu All Over Again": Eight Types of Tautology. *Et Cetera – A Review of General Semantics*, 58, 151–165.

Moore, M. (2003) *Measure for Measure: Essays on Tests, Evaluation, and Research*, Haifa: Michlol – Academia. (In Hebrew)

Moore, M. and Kramer, D. (2000) We Are Too Weak to Walk Unaided: A Family Therapist View of the Pathogenic Aspects of Prayer. *Modern Library*, www.infidels.org/library/modern/michael_moore/weak.html (accessed November 11, 2011).

Morman, M. T. and Floyd, K. (2006) Sonhood: Defining What it Means to be a Good Son, in *Widening the Family Circle: New Research on Family Communication* (eds K. Floyd and M. T. Morman), Thousand Oaks, CA: Sage, pp. 37–55.

Myerson, R. B. (1991) *Game Theory – Analysis of Conflict*, Cambridge, MA: Harvard University Press.

Nail, P. R. and Van Leeuwen, M. D. (1993) An Analysis and Restructuring of the Diamond Model of Social Response. *Personality and Social Psychology Bulletin*, 19, 106–116.

Nichols, M. P. (2009) *Family Therapy – Concepts and Methods*, 9th edn, Upper Saddle River, NJ: Prentice Hall.

Nichols, M. P. and Schwartz, R. C. (2006) *Family Therapy: Concepts and Methods*, 7th edn, Boston, MA: Pearson.

NIDA (2008) Brief Strategic Family Therapy for Adolescent Drug Abuse. www.drugabuse.gov/TXManuals/BSFT/BSFT4.html (accessed November 11, 2011).

Olson, D. H. (2000) Circumplex Model of Marital and Family Systems. *Journal of Family Therapy*, 22, 144–167.

ONS (Office for National Statistics) (2009) *Marriage, Divorce and Adoption Statistics*, Series FM2, no. 34. Crown Copyright.

Peleg, O. (2008) The Relation between Differentiation of Self and Marital Satisfaction: What Can be Learned from Married People Over the Course of Life? *The American Journal of Family Therapy*, 36, 388–401.

Perls, F. S., Hefferline, R. F., and Goodman, P. (1973) *Gestalt Therapy*, Harmondsworth, Middlesex: Penguin.

Piliavin, J. A. (2008) Long-term Benefits of Habitual Helping – Doing Well by Doing Good, in *Cooperation – The Political Psychology of Effective Human Interaction* (eds B. A. Sullivan, M. Snyder, and J. L. Sullivan), Malden, MA: Blackwell, pp. 241–258.

Pincus, L. and Dare, C. (1978) *Secrets in the Family: A Psychodynamic Approach to the Unconscious Beliefs, Longings and Incestuous Fantasies that Shape Family Relationships*. New York: Pantheon.

Pollastri, A. R., Cardemil, E. V., and O'Donnell, E. H. (2010) Self-esteem in Pure Bullies and Bully/Victims: Longitudinal Analysis. *Journal of Interpersonal Violence*, 20, 1–14.

Popenoe, D. and Whitehead, B. D. (2007) The State of our Unions: The Social Health of Marriage in America. *The National Marriage Project*, Rutgers, NJ: The State University of New Jersey.

Pratt, M. W., Kerig, P. K., Cowan, P. A., and Cowan, C. P. (1992) Family Worlds: Couple Satisfaction, Parenting Style, and Mothers' and Fathers' Speech to Young Children. *Merrill-Palmer Quarterly*, 38, 245–262.

Pribor, E. F. and Dinwiddie, S. H. (1992) Psychiatric Correlates of Incest in Childhood. *American Journal of Psychiatry*, 149, 52–56.

Reischauer, E. D. (1977) *The Japanese*, Cambridge, MA: Harvard University Press.

Reyome, N. D. and Ward, K. S. (2007) Self-reported History of Childhood Maltreatment and Codependency in Undergraduate Nursing Students. *Journal of Emotional Abuse*, 7, 37–50.

Rogers, C. (1967) *On Becoming a Person – A Therapist's View of Psychotherapy*, London: Constable.

Rogers, C. (1972) The Person of Tomorrow, in *Marriage and Family in a Decade of Change* (ed G. B. Carr), Reading, MA: Addison-Wesley, pp. 3–8.

Rogers, C. (1980) *A Way of Being*, Boston: Houghton Mifflin.

Rogers, C. (1990a) Client-centered Therapy, in *Carl Rogers: Dialogues* (eds H. Kirschenbaum and V. L. Henderson), London: Constable, pp. 9–38.

Rogers, C. (1990b) The Necessary and Sufficient Conditions of Therapeutic Personality Change, in *The Carl Rogers Reader* (eds H. Kirschenbaum and V. L. Henderson), London: Constable, pp. 219–235.

Rogers, C. (1990c) A Theory of Therapy, Personality, and Interpersonal Relationships, as Developed in the Client-centered Framework, in *The Carl Rogers Reader* (eds H. Kirschenbaum and V. L. Henderson), London: Constable, pp. 236–257.

Rogers, C. (1990d) Do We Need "a" Reality? in *The Carl Rogers Reader* (eds H. Kirschenbaum and V. L. Henderson), London: Constable, pp. 420–429.

Rogers, C. (1990e) The Directive Versus the Nondirective Approach in *The Carl Rogers Reader* (eds H. Kirschenbaum and V. L. Henderson), London: Constable, pp. 77–87.

Rosenzweig, S. (1988) Revised Norms for the Children's Form of the Rosenzweig Picture-Frustration (P-F) Study, with Updated P-F Reference List. *Journal of Clinical Child Psychology*, 17, 326–328.

Roth, P. (1968) *When She Was Good*, New York: Bantam.

Rubin, Z. and Peplau, L. A. (1975) Who Believes in a Just World? *Journal of Social Issues*, 31(3), 65–89.

Ryan, W. (1976) *Blaming the Victim*, rev. edn, New York: Vintage.

Saramago, J. (1998) *Blindness*, New York: Harcourt.

Satir, V. (1983) *Conjoint Family Therapy*, 3rd rev. edn, Palo Alto, CA: Science and Behavior Books.

Satir, V. (1988) *The New Peoplemaking*, Mountain View, CA: Science and Behavior Books.

Scanzoni, J. (1972) *Sexual Bargaining – Power Politics in the American Marriage*, Englewood Cliffs, NJ: Prentice Hall.

Schaffer, M., Clark, S., and Jeglic, E. L. (2008) The Role of Empathy and Parenting Style in the Development of Antisocial Behaviors. *Crime and Delinquency*, 55, 586–599.

Schreier, A., Wolke, D., Thomas, K., Horwood, J., Hollis, C., Gunnell, D., Lewis, G., Thompson, A., Zammit, S., Duffy, L., Salvi, G., and Harrison, G. (2009) Prospective Study of Peer Victimization in Childhood and Psychotic Symptoms in a Nonclinical Population at Age 12 Years. *Archives of General Psychiatry*, 66, 527–536.

Schwebel, A. (1993) Family Defense Mechanisms: The Concept and the Utility to Family Scientists, Practitioners, and Educators. *The Family Journal*, 31, 31–41.

Seikkula, L. (2002) Open Dialogues with Good and Poor Outcomes for Psychotic Crises: Examples from Families with Violence. *Journal of Marital and Family Therapy*, 28, 263–274.

Seligman, M. E. P. (2002) Positive Psychology, Positive Prevention, and Positive Therapy, in *Handbook of Positive Psychology* (eds R. Snyder and S. J. Lopez), Oxford: Oxford University Press, pp. 3–12.

Smith, P. K., Shu, S., and Madsen, K. (2001) Characteristics of Victims of School Bullying – Developmental Changes in Coping Strategies and Skills, in *Peer Harassment in School: The Plight of the Vulnerable and Victimized* (eds J. Juvonen and S. Graham), New York: The Guilford Press, pp. 332–352.

Sommers-Flanagan, J. and Sommers-Flanagan, R. (2009) *Clinical Interviewing*, 4th edn, Hoboken, NJ: Wiley.

Springer, C. A., Britt, T. W., and Schlenker, B. R. (1998) Codependency: Clarifying the Construct. *Journal of Mental Health Counseling*, 20, 141–158.

Stagner, R. (1951) Homeostasis as a Unifying Concept in Personality Theory. *Psychological Review*, 58, 5–17.

Stagner, R. (1977) Homeostasis, Discrepancy, Dissonance: A Theory of Motives and Motivation. *Motivation and Emotion*, 1, 103–138.

Stewart, I. and Joines, V. (1987) *TA Today – A New Introduction to Transactional Analysis*, Nottingham: Lifespace Publishing.

Stirling, J. Jr. and the Committee on Child Abuse and Neglect (2007) Beyond Munchausen Syndrome by Proxy: Identification and Treatment of Child Abuse in a Medical Setting. *Pediatrics*, 119, 1026–1030.

Straffin, P. D. (2004) *Game Theory and Strategy*, Washington, DC: The Mathematical Association of America.

Straus, M. A. (1996) Spanking and the Making of a Violent Society. *Pediatrics*, 98, 837–842.

Sue, D. W. and Sue, D. (2008) *Counseling the Culturally Diverse: Theory and Practice*, 5th edn, Hoboken, NJ: Wiley.

Sullivan, B. A., Snyder, M., and Sullivan, J. L. (2008) The Centrality of Cooperation in the Functioning of Individuals and Groups, in *Cooperation – The Political*

Psychology of Effective Human Interaction (eds B. A. Sullivan, M. Snyder, and J. L. Sullivan), Malden, MA: Blackwell, pp. 1–16.

Suls, J., Martin, R., and Wheeler, L. (2002) Social Comparison: Why, With Whom, and With What Effect? *Current Directions in Psychological Science*, 11, 159–163.

Tatar, M. (1992) *Off With Their Heads! Fairy Tales and the Culture of Childhood*, Princeton, NJ: Princeton University Press.

Taylor, C. (1991) *The Ethics of Authenticity*, Cambridge, MA: Harvard University Press.

These Last Days Ministries (2010) www.tldm.org/default.htm (accessed November 11, 2011).

Time Magazine (1998) 151, No. 25, p. 15.

Toufexis, A. (1996) Why Jennifer Got Sick. *Time Magazine*, April 29.

Trenholm, S. and Jensen, A. (2004) *Interpersonal Communication*, New York: Oxford University Press.

Triandis, H. C. (1991) Cross-cultural Differences in Assertiveness/Competition vs. Group Loyalty/Cooperation, in *Cooperation and Prosocial Behaviour* (eds R. A. Hinde and J. Groebel), Cambridge: Cambridge University Press, pp. 78–88.

Triandis, H. C. (1995) *Individualism and Collectivism*, Boulder, CO: Westview Press.

Trilling, L. (1972) *Sincerity and Authenticity*, London: Oxford University Press.

Tudor, K. (1999) *Group Counselling*, London: Sage.

Turner, E. A., Chandler, M., and Heffer, R. W. (2009) The Influence of Parenting Styles, Achievement Motivation, and Self-efficacy on Academic Performance in College Students. *Journal of College Student Development*, 50, 337–346.

Turner, M., Pratkanis, A. R., and Struckman, C. (2007) Groupthink as Social Identity Maintenance, in *The Science of Social Influence: Advances and Future Progress* (ed. A. R. Pratkanis), New York: Psychology Press, pp. 223–246.

United Nations (1950) *Yearbook of the United Nations – 1948–49*. New York: United Nations.

Valesio, P. (1980) *Novantiqua*, Bloomington, IN: Indiana University Press.

Wang, Q., Bowling, N. A., and Eschleman, K. J. (2010) A Meta-analytic Examination of Work and General Locus of Control. *Journal of Applied Psychology*, 95, 761–768.

Weldon, F. (1981) Man With No Eyes, in *Watching Me, Watching You and Other Stories*, London: Hodder and Stoughton, pp. 60–84.

White, M. (2007) *Maps of Narrative Practice*, New York: Norton.

Williams, T. (1957) *Cat On a Hot Tin Roof*, Harmondsworth: Penguin.

Wolke, D. and Skew, A. (2011) Bullied at Home and at School: Relationship to Behaviour Problems and Unhappiness, in *Understanding Society: Early Findings from the First Wave of the UK's Household Longitudinal Study*, www.understandingsociety.org.uk/ (accessed November 11, 2011).

Wood, A. M., Linley, P. A., Maltby, J., Baliousis, M., and Joseph, S. (2008) The Authentic Personality: A Theoretical and Empirical Conceptualization and the

Development of the Authenticity Scale. *Journal of Counseling Psychology*, 55, 385–399.

World Health Organization (2004) *Health Behavior in School-aged Children*, Fact Sheet EURO/04/04. Copenhagen: WHO Europe.

Wright, R. (2000) *Nonzero: The Logic of Human Destiny*, London: Little, Brown.

Wynne, L., Ryckoff, I. M., Day, J., and Hirsch, S. I. (1958) Pseudomutuality in the Family Relationships of Schizophrenics. *Psychiatry*, 21, 205–220.

Yalom, I. D. (1991) *Love's Executioner and Other Tales of Psychotherapy*, London: Penguin.

Yalom, I. D. (1993) *When Nietzsche Wept*, New York: Harper.

Yalom, I. D. (1995) *Theory and Practice of Group Psychotherapy*, New York: Basic Books.

Yalom, I. D. (1997) *Lying on the Couch*, New York: HarperCollins.

Index

Destructive Myths in Family Therapy: How to Overcome Barriers to Communication by Seeing and Saying – A Humanistic Perspective, First Edition. Daniela Kramer-Moore and Michael Moore.
© 2012 John Wiley & Sons, Ltd. Published 2012 by John Wiley & Sons, Ltd.